EXPLORING
SPELLCRAFT

HOW TO
Create AND
Cast
Effective
Spells

GERINA DUNWICH

NEW PAGE BOOKS
A division of The Career Press, Inc.
Franklin Lakes, NJ

EXPLORING SPELLCRAFT
Cover design by Lu Rossman
Printed in the U.S.A. by Book-mart Press

To order this title, please call toll-free 1-800-CAREER-1 (NJ and Canada: 201-848-0310) to order using VISA or MasterCard, or for further information on books from Career Press.

The Career Press, Inc., 3 Tice Road, PO Box 687,
Franklin Lakes, NJ 07417
www.newpagebooks.com
www.careerpress.com

Library of Congress Cataloging-in-Publication Data
Dunwich, Gerina.
    Exploring spellcraft : how to create and cast effective spells
/ by Gerina Dunwich.
        p. cm.
    Includes bibliographical references and index.
    ISBN 1-56414-494-1 (paper)
        1. Witchcraft. 2. Charms. 3. Magic. I. Title.

BF1566 .D866 2001
133.4'4—dc21

00-050710

With an abundance of love and gratitude do I hereby dedicate this book to Al, to my mother, to all of my sisters and brothers in the Craft, and to my beloved goddess Bast.

Many thanks and bright blessings to Stephany Evans and Mike Lewis for helping to make this book possible, and to Sybil, Scott, and Doreen for their invaluable inspiration and guidance from beyond.

And to my good friends at Panpipes Magickal Marketplace in Hollywood, California, a very special thank you for graciously allowing me to borrow items from your shop to use in the photographs that were taken for this book.

Blessed Be!

Contents

Introduction   9

Chapter 1
Crafting the Magick   11

Chapter 2
Magickal Correspondences   32

Chapter 3
A Time for Magick   39

Chapter 4
Divination Before Incantation   61

Chapter 5
Amulets, Talismans, Charms,   78
and Fetishes

Chapter 6
the Magick of Wax and Wick   92

Chapter 7
A Book of Shadows   110

Chapter 8
Fertility Magick   126

Chapter 9
Weatherworking   133

Chapter 10
A Kitchen Witch's Miscellanea   142

Chapter 11
Yuletide Witches, Superstitions,   168
and Spells

Chapter 12
Sybil Leek   176

Chapter 13
Black Magick   183

Afterword   206

Resources   211

Bibliography   214

Index   217

I Am a Witch

I am a Witch
With rhymes and reasons.
I am a changeling like the seasons.
My mother is the Moon,
My father is the Sun;
With Goddess Earth am I as one.
I am a Witch, a Pagan child.
Mother Nature's spirit so wild
Grows within me,
Flows within me,
Meandering like a spellbound stream,
Enchanting my every waking dream.
I breathe the air of liberation,
I tend the fire of transformation,
I drink the water of creation,
Earth-magick is my conjuration.
I am a Witch of shadow and light,
Of Avalon mists and ravens' flight.
I am a Witch, with pride say I,
For a Witch's soul
Does never die.

—Gerina Dunwich

Introduction

The casting of spells is an art that can bestow upon you many of the things in life that you need and desire. Since ancient times, this art has played an important role in many of the cultures and religions throughout the world. Along with the worship of the old gods, spellcrafting was (and still is) an important aspect of the Old Religion known as Witchcraft, the Craft of the Wise, or the pre-Christian Religion of the Earth.

As the Age of Aquarius dawns in the new millennium, and the world bears witness to a resurgence of Paganism and an ever-growing spiritual reconnection to the Old Ways, an increasing number of persons of all ages and from all walks of life are finding themselves drawn to the magickal arts.

A spell, which some refer to as a Witch's prayer, is not the work of the Devil. Nor is it only under the domain of those who are gifted with psychic or supernatural powers. Nearly anyone can learn how to cast a spell. Just as Traditional Witches can be of any religion or even hold agnostic or atheistic views, so too can a spellcrafter be of any religious or non-religious path. One does not need to be initiated into any mystery cults, swear an oath of dedication to any god or goddess, denounce or convert to any religion, or even wear the label of a Witch or Wiccan in order to be a spellcrafter. But among the things that are required, the most important ones are an open mind, true desire and will, patience, self-conviction, the courage to follow what is within one's heart, and the maturity to take responsibility for one's own actions.

Spells need not be complicated or involve expensive and hard-to-find paraphernalia in order to achieve positive results. The real magick, as any Witch or practitioner knows, comes from within.

Once you gain an understanding of how magickal energy works and learn the secrets to casting spells, you will be able to tap into your inner powers, focus, and direct them utilizing simple items found in the average home or easily purchased at the nearest occult shop. In fact, many of the herbs and other ingredients called for in spells can be found right in your very own kitchen!

This book is designed to be a guide to the history, philosophy, ethics, and practical application of spellcrafting. Written with the novice-to-intermediate student in mind, it covers all areas of folk magick in an explorative and non-biased manner.

Chapter 1

Crafting the Magick

The Tools of the Trade

The basic tools (also known as "weapons") of spellcraft include the athame, wand, sword, pentacle, cords, cauldron, chalice, and altar bell—all of which are traditionally cleansed and then enchanted (or "charged") by the practitioner prior to use.

Many spellcrafters feel that the best ritual tools are the ones that a magickal practitioner personally fashions for his or her own use, or the ones that are received as gifts. Other practitioners have no objections to purchasing their tools new at an occult shop; however, it is an old magickal custom when buying magickal tools or ingredients for a spell to never argue with the merchant over the price. To do so is said to cause the buyer to be jinxed. In addition, many Witches fear that their rituals tools and magickal supplies will not work properly or, in some cases, will be completely ineffective in magickal workings, should they haggle over their marked prices.

To steal a ritual tool, or any object handcrafted or owned by a Witch or magician, according to an ancient legend, brings down a powerful curse upon the thief, which he or she can never be free of until the stolen property is returned to its rightful owner. Only then can the curse be lifted.

The Athame

The athame is a ritual dagger with a double-edged blade and a black (sometimes white) handle, which many Witches paint or engrave with runic names and magickal symbols. It is employed for casting the circle, the storing and directing of magickal energy during rituals, the stirring of potions, the ritual mixing of salt and water, inscribing the magick circle, and the consecration and charging of such things as poppets, mojo bags, and amuletic or talismanic objects. In addition, the athame is used in both invocations and evocations, initiation ceremonies, pentagram rituals (invoking and banishing), the calling of the Lords of the Watchtowers, and many other rites and spellcastings.

In certain traditions of Wicca, the athame is never used for cutting or for any purpose that is mundane (non-magickal). However, there are many Witches and other magickal folks who use their athames as often as possible, both in and out of the circle, in the old belief that an athame's power increases with use. If one chooses to restrict the use of his or her athame only to the casting of circles or certain ritual work, that is fine. But if spellcraft is looked at from a historic point of view, one will find that the women and men of the old Pagan religions commonly used for magickal workings the same knife that they used for harvesting herbs, hunting, food preparation, and even self-defense.

The Wand

The traditional uses of the wand are to cast the circle, draw magickal symbols on the ground, invoke spirits, conduct spiritual energy, and stir cauldron brews. Some magickal practitioners also use a wand for manifestation, which is the ritual transformation of spirit into matter.

The wand is an instrument traditionally carved from the wood of the hazel, ash, rowan, or willow tree. Some modern Witches' wands are fashioned from crystal, carved ivory or ebony, or metal such as silver or gold.

To Witches and ceremonial magicians, the wand is the emblem of power and the life-force. It symbolizes the ancient element of Air (in some traditions it symbolizes Fire), and is said to be sacred to all gods and goddesses of the Pagan pantheons.

The Sword

The sword is a tool used more frequently by ceremonial magicians and Witchcraft covens than by solitary practitioners of the Craft. In many traditions of Wicca, the sword is used in the same manner as the athame, but it is considered to be more authoritative. It is also used for invoking the Lords of the Watchtowers and for making salutations. And like the athame, the sword is typically engraved with runic names and magickal symbols.

The Pentacle

The pentacle is a flat disc of wood, wax, copper, silver, clay, or glass bearing the motif of the five-pointed star known as the pentagram. The pentacle is found on the altars of many Wiccans. Representing female/Goddess energy and the ancient Element of Earth, its main uses are aiding meditation, invoking spirits, protection against evil entities, and grounding energy after rituals and spells have been performed. Some covens also use the pentacle to serve food during "Cakes and Wine" ceremonies, which traditionally follow Sabbats and esbats.

The Cord

Cords are used by many Witches and covens as tools to store magickal energy for later use. In traditional cord-magick, nine knots are tied in certain patterns or orders in a cord while an incantation is chanted and one's intent is visualized. When the Witch is ready to release the power that has been stored within the cord, he or she then unties the knots in the same order in which they were tied. Many Witches untie one knot each night for nine nights in a row.

The Cauldron

Since ancient times the cauldron has been linked to Witches and various Pagan deities. Traditionally made of iron (a metal that naturally repels all manner of evil), the cauldron possesses great mystical power and feminine energy. It symbolically combines the influences of the four ancient Elements of Air, Fire, Water, and Earth, and its three legs symbolize the three phases of the moon (waxing, full, and waning); the past, present, and future; or the triad of body, mind, and spirit. For many Wiccans, the cauldron represents the dark and divine womb of the Mother Goddess, and its three legs the three Goddess aspects of Maiden, Mother, and Crone. Cauldrons are used for various purposes, including alchemy, fire rituals, scrying, raising storms, brewing potions, burning incense, and holding charcoal blocks, votive candles, amulets, talismans, and herbs.

The Chalice

The chalice, or sacred goblet, is a tool corresponding to the Element of Water and possessing strong feminine energy. It is traditionally made of silver (a metal magickally corresponding to the energies of the moon); however, some are made of glass, crystal, wood, pewter, bronze, or gold. Plastic is never used.

Many Witches use chalices for the ritual mixing of salt and water, the blending of magick potions, and the pouring of libations. In the Wiccan ritual known as the symbolic Great Rite (the powerful rite of sexual intercourse) the chalice is used to represent the yoni of the Goddess. In Cakes and Wine ceremonies, it is traditional for a chalice to be filled with wine and then passed around in a clockwise circle from coven member to coven member, who each partake of it.

The Altar Bell

In some Wiccan traditions, a small bell is kept on the altar and rung three times to signal the start or close of a ritual. Bells are also used by Witches and other practitioners of magick to both summon and banish spirits and entities, dispel negative vibrations and evil influences, drive away mischievous fairies, and, according to Rosemary Ellen Guiley in *The Encyclopedia of Witches and Witchcraft,* "enhance harmony and augment power.

Since ancient times bells have been employed as charms to promote fertility, avert the evil eye, and bring forth the rain. The drinking of wine, holy water, or sacrificial blood from an inverted bell was at one time thought to possess great curative powers.

In the practices of Voodoo, Santeria, and many African religions, bells are often rung to invoke deities. In Shamanism, they have long been used to keep evil spirits at bay, and in the Middle Ages they played an important role in necromantic rites to summon the dead from their graves.

Other important tools of spellcraft include candles, incense, and magickal oils all of which will be discussed in more detail in later chapters.

Crafting Thine Own Spells

There are two ways to craft your own spells. The first is to take an existing spell and personalize it to suit your individual needs. Ingredients such as herbs and oils can easily be modified (as long as their magickal properties correspond to your intent), incantations can be reworded, deities can often be substituted to accommodate your personal spiritual tradition or cultural/ethnic heritage, and so forth. Feel free to add, omit, and change until the spell becomes yours. The idea behind personalization is to put as much of your energies into the spell as possible, while at the same time retaining its original structure.

The second way is to create a new spell completely from scratch. Many Witches do this when they are unable to find an appropriate spell for their need or desire, or when the spells crafted by others just don't feel right. The first step is to research the magickal correspondences to find the herbs, deities, colors, planets, Elements, and other things that relate to your intent, and then decide which of them you want to work with. The more magickal correspondences you incorporate into your spellwork, the more potent your magick will be.

The next step is to write an incantation that clearly states your need or desire. Incantations can be either simple or poetic, and they may also include an invocation to a deity if you should so desire. Rhyming incantations are not only traditional, but they are said to be more powerful because of their magick-making rhythm. The Rede of the Wiccae, written by Lady Gwen Thompson and published in the Spring 1975 issue of *The Green Egg,* supports this with the following lines: "To bind the spell every time, let the spell be spake in rhyme."

It matters not if you are a great poet so long as there is intent behind your words. It is a spellcaster's intent and will, combined with the energy that he or she raises and sends forth, that fuels a spell. Incantations, along with candles, incense, robes, and ritual tools, do not, in themselves, possess the power to create magick. The true magick comes from the heart and soul of the practitioner.

The final step is to determine the appropriate time for casting your spell. Remember that working in harmony with the phases of the moon, astrological influences, and planetary hours will add additional energy to your magick.

Working In Harmony with the 4 Elements

Believed to have been designated by the ancient Sumerians, and also said to have been created by the goddess Kali, the four Elements of Air, Fire, Water, and Earth possess great power in their symbolism. Some magickal traditions regard the Elements as fivefold, with the fifth Element being Ether—a "non-material" of which astral bodies, spirits, angels, and deities are made.

It was the Greco-Roman philosophical sect known as the Stoics who assigned zodiac signs, seasons, colors, and gods and goddesses to each of the four Elements. The Roman deities traditionally connected with Air, Fire, Water, and Earth are Saturn, Mars, Venus, and Jupiter, respectively. However, with the exception of Mars, the planets correspond to different Elements than the Roman deities whose names they bear.

The four Elements have long played an important role in the practices of magick and Witchcraft. They are said to form the foundation of natural magick, and their forces and guardian spirits are often invoked by Witches prior to a ritual or the casting of a spell. Each cardinal point of a magick circle corresponds to one of the Elements (East-Air; South-Fire; West-Water; and North-Earth), and in both Witchcraft and ceremonial magic, ritual tools are traditionally consecrated with the symbols of the Elements: incense or breath (Air); candle flame (Fire); water (Water); and salt or pentacle (Earth).

Air and Its Elementals

The Element of Air represents the mind, and the metaphysical principle that it reflects is that of Life. It corresponds to the East, Spring Equinox, the planets Mercury and Uranus, the masculine forces of Nature, yang energy, positive polarity, the metal silver, the Tarot suit of Swords, the color yellow, and the astrological signs of Aquarius, Gemini, and Libra.

The Air Element is personified by low-level spiritual beings (Elementals) known as Sylphs. They are traditionally connected with the East quarter (or watchtower) of the ritual circle, and often appear as tiny winged creatures with facial features that vaguely resemble those of humans. They are almost transparent and have been described as ethereal butterflies by gifted individuals who have seen or psychically perceived them.

The ruler of this Elemental race is a higher being, or guardian, called Paralda. In certain traditions of Wicca, the ruler of the Sylphs is called Eurus, whose name is taken from the Roman god of the East wind. Air Elementals may be invoked to increase energy (physical or magickal) and stimulate the powers of the intellect. Their energy greatly enhances all spells and rituals involving new beginnings, spiritual liberation, organization, divination, travel, writing, creation, and communication.

Fire and Its Elementals

The Element of Fire represents the spirit, and the metaphysical principle that it reflects is that of Light. It corresponds to the South, Summer Solstice, the Sun and the planets Mars and Jupiter, the masculine forces of Nature, yang energy, positive polarity, the metal gold, the Tarot suit of Wands, the color red or orange, and the astrological signs Aries, Leo, and Sagittarius.

The Fire Element is personified by low-level spiritual beings (Elementals) known as Salamanders. They are traditionally connected with the South quarter (or watchtower) of the ritual circle, and they resemble newt-like creatures. They sometimes have red scales and wings of fire, and are usually found in and around the flames of candles used in Pagan rituals or spellcastings. They are extremely powerful and should always be treated with both respect and caution, and should be formally banished after ritual work has been completed. To banish a Salamander, point the tip of your athame at the southern quadrant of the circle and visualize the Elemental returning from where it came from. As you do this, give thanks to it for its blessings and protection, and then bid it hail and farewell.

The ruler of this Elemental race is a higher being, or guardian, called Djin. In certain Wiccan traditions, the ruler of the

Salamanders is called Notus, whose name is taken from the Roman god of the South wind. Fire Elementals are beneficent for spellcraft that involves sexuality, courage, success, dowsing, strength, protection, and the banishing of illness, jealousy, and anger.

Water and Its Elementals

The Element of Water represents the soul and the emotions, and the metaphysical principle that it reflects is that of Love. It corresponds to the West, Autumn Equinox, the Moon and the planets Neptune and Pluto, the feminine forces of Nature, yin energy, negative polarity, the metal silver, the Tarot suit of Cups, the color blue, and the astrological signs Pisces, Cancer, and Scorpio.

The Water Element is personified by low-level spiritual beings (elementals) known as Undines. They are traditionally connected with the West quarter (or watchtower) of the ritual circle, and have been described as tiny creatures resembling seahorses with human-like faces. According to ancient Greek folklore, they were water sprites who inhabited the Aegean Sea. Their name derives from the Latin word unda, meaning wave.

The ruler of this Elemental race is a higher being, or guardian, called Necksa. In certain Wiccan traditions, the ruler of the Undines is called Zephyrus, whose name is taken from the Roman god of the West wind. Water Elementals may be invoked to strengthen clairvoyance, restore emotional balance, and aid meditation. All rituals and spells involving love, partnerships, children, or the home are greatly enhanced by the presence of the Undines.

Earth and Its Elementals

The Element of Earth represents the physical body, and the metaphysical principle that it reflects is that of Law. It corresponds to the North, Winter Solstice, the planets Earth, Venus, and Saturn, the feminine forces of Nature, yin energy, negative polarity, the metal gold, the Tarot suit of Pentacles, the color green, and the astrological signs Taurus, Virgo, and Capricorn.

The Earth Element is personified by low-level spiritual beings (Elementals) known as Gnomes. They are traditionally connected with the North quarter (or watchtower) of the ritual circle, and often appear as hirsute, dwarf-like creatures with aged features. They dwell deep within forests, particularly in or under old oak trees.

The ruler of this Elemental race is a higher being, or guardian, called Gob. In certain Wiccan traditions, the ruler of the Gnomes is called Boreas, whose name is taken from the Roman god of the North wind. Earth Elementals may be invoked for protection and healing, especially of animals. Their energy enhances herb-magick and spells involving fertility, nature, money, agriculture, careers, and business. Additionally, all Gaia-healings and rituals honoring woodland deities are made even more magickally powerful when the forces of the Gnomes are summoned.

The Ethics of Love Magick: One Witch's Perspective

Many individuals who follow the path of Wicca are concerned about casting love spells that may, in the end, manipulate the free will of another human being. In order to work magick and remain within the parameters of their ethics, Wiccans will frequently direct a spell at a situation and not at a person, attach contingencies to their incantations (such as "harming none," "for the good of all," or "interfering with the free will of none"), cast love-drawing spells in which a particular person is neither named nor visualized, or acquire an individual's permission before casting a spell that involves him or her.

Most Wiccans feel that love magick should not be taken lightly (which I am in total agreement with), and some are vehemently opposed to its use in any capacity. I have even heard some erroneously categorize it as "black magick," which I find to be a rather absurd deduction. Some of the more manipulative forms of love magick may border on being "gray," if you feel a need to attach a color to it, but love spells are by no means black magick—unless, of course, the intent behind the spell is to somehow bring harm to the person at whom it is directed.

An example of a true "black magick love spell" would be one intended to break up someone's marriage or eliminate someone's lover in order to put yourself in a more favorable position to win the heart of the man or woman who is your love interest. (Let it be noted that this is definitely not the sort of love magick that I would practice, advocate, or teach to my students.)

Personally, and I speak as a Witch and not a Wiccan, I am not opposed to love magick, and I fail to see much difference between the lovelorn woman who uses a positive spell to influence the affections of a particular man and the woman who uses her feminine wiles (and anything else she might have in her arsenal) to accomplish the same thing. Both methods are manipulative to one degree or another, and both may be necessary to get Cupid's arrow pointed in the right direction.

However, where using magick to dominate the free will of someone else is concerned, I have always been of the opinion that it is an impossibility to completely control the will of another, unless that person gives you the power to do so. I also firmly believe that no amount of love magick can force another person to fall wildly in love with you against his own free will, even if you utter that person's name or visualize his physical features during your spellcasting (contrary to what many Wiccans seem to think). Even if you go to the lengths of working a love charm involving the hair or fingernail clippings of your love interest (which happens to be a very common magickal practice outside of Wicca), the most that love magick can do is create a spark between two people. It is up to them at that point whether or not it turns into a blazing fire. If their romantic feelings for each other are not mutual, the spark will eventually burn itself out and thus the spell will, figuratively speaking, turn into dust and blow away.

Frequently Asked Questions

What is magick and how does it work?

Magick has been described and theorized in a number of different ways by many different people. Aleister Crowley's concise definition of magick as "the science and art of causing change to occur in conformity to the will" has irrefutably been the most noted since the year 1929, when it was published in Crowley's classic work, *Magick in Theory and Practice.* Crowley also said that every intentional act was an act of magick.

Harry E. Wedeck, the author of *A Treasury of Witchcraft,* describes magick as "the imposition of the human will on the phenomena of nature," and Martin Delrio (a medieval demonology author) defined it as "an art or skill that, by means of a not supernatural force, produces certain strange and unusual phenomena whose rationale eludes common sense."

My personal definition and concise theory of magick is as follows: Magick is the ritual use of the Three Powers (the power of the human will, the power of intent, and the power of visualization) to bring about either positive or negative transformations and manifestations. Spells and rituals are used as tools to channel the power of this magick in the desired direction.

In their book *The Supernatural,* Douglas Hill and Pat Williams write, "The power of the spell derives from the power of words and of incantations." When a spell is put to paper it "may appear prosaic or repetitive, but its effectiveness lies in its associations and in its method of delivery, and in the repetition of ritual that allows its impact to be built up and reinforced. Secrecy is also an important factor in spells."

How long does it take for a spell to work?

All spells, just as all spellcrafters, are different, and the length of time it takes for one spell to take effect may be longer or shorter from one to another. If a spell is carried out according to its instructions during the most favorable lunar phase and planetary hour, and the spellcrafter's will and visualization skills are strong, the results of the spell may be seen or felt anywhere from instantaneously to within one complete monthly lunar cycle. Somewhere in the middle (about two weeks) is probably the average time it takes for a spell to work, although I have heard of certain spells that have taken up to six months to come to fruition, and one that required a year and one day.

Sometimes a spell must be repeated more than once before it works. Have patience and do not give up, especially if you are a novice spellcrafter and are unsuccessful in the beginning. Remember the old adage that "practice makes perfect." The more you work with magick, the more finely tuned and powerful your magickal skills will eventually become.

Can a spell be made to work every time?

It would be a perfect world indeed if all of our spells worked all of the time. Unfortunately, this is not the way it is for any practitioner of the magickal arts.

There are many different factors that can contribute to the success or failure of a spell, such as willpower, visualization, lunar and planetary influences, and magickal correspondences, just to name a few. If a spell is worked improperly, if your energy level is not up to par, if your timing is off, or if powerful outside forces (such as another spellcrafter's counter-magick) are working against you, there is a good chance that your spellwork will fail or, at the very least, be weakened and/or delayed in reaching its mark. Also, not all spells will work the same way for all spellcrafters. It is often necessary for one to experiment with different spells until the right one comes along and the magickal energies between spellcrafter and spell spark and ignite.

Some spells seem to naturally work better than others, and the more power that is put into a spell, the greater its chances of success are. Therefore, if your magickal working concerns any personal issue that you feel very strongly about, it would most certainly be to your benefit to cast the spell yourself rather than to rely on another spellcrafter, who may not invest the same amount of emotional intensity into the spell as you would.

Remember the next time you open a book of magick—whether it is an ancient grimoire, a Witchcraft spellbook, or a Wiccan's Book of Shadows—that you are merging yourself with works that were created by other people whose personal energies are contained within their written words and ideas. As a spellcrafter, you may find that these energies are compatible with yours and you may even find yourself drawing power from them. Or, as sometimes the case may be, a negative energy clash may result and prevent the spell from working for you no matter how hard you try or how many times you attempt it. This is why many Witches prefer composing their own spells and rituals to working with those penned by others.

Can spells be reversed, and how is this accomplished?

Some spells may be more difficult to reverse than others, but just about any spell can be reversed if the right technique is applied.

There are a number of ways to reverse a spell. The recasting of one's original spell in a reversed fashion, with its incantation recited backwards is a method that has been used by Witches for centuries. Another method is to cast a spell known as a "spellbreaker" to eliminate the original spell (see Chapter 13). These are traditionally carried out when the moon is on the wane. Spellbreakers can also be employed for spells cast by others, although reversing such spells often requires considerably more energy and time than reversing those of your own casting—especially if the other person is deliberately working his magick against you.

There is an old saying among Witches that "The only way to bring a spell to an end is with another spell," but this is not necessarily true. Very few spells are ever permanent. Most that are cast need to be periodically renewed in order to keep on working. If they are not renewed, their magickal effects gradually dissipate until they are eventually no more.

Can love magick be used on members of the same sex?

Yes and no. Love magick can work for gays and lesbians in precisely the same way that it works for heterosexuals, and with a minimal amount of alteration, most "straight" love spells can be adapted to suit the needs of gays and lesbians. For example, the herbs and oils used in a spell involving love between two men should all possess masculine energy, and if candle magick is employed, two male-shaped or two phallus candles should be burned upon the altar in place of a male and a female one, which are often called for in candle magick rituals involving heterosexual love.

In the case of bisexual men or women, love magick can be used to attract a partner of either gender who may be either gay, straight, or bisexual. However, love magick cannot be used to romantically or sexually draw straight people to gay people. Magick should never be worked with the intent to altar someone's natural sexuality, whether it be gay, straight, or what have you. There are many things that magick can make possible, but this is not one of them. If you are strongly attracted to a man or a woman who does not share your sexuality, it would behoove you to simply accept this person for who and what he or she are and redirect your energies to find yourself a more compatible love mate.

Does the Devil ever play a role in the art of spellcrafting?

The Devil, as defined by Christianity, plays no role whatsoever in either the magickal or religious practices of modern Witches, Druids, Shamans, Neo-Pagans, or any of the diverse traditions that exist within Wicca. Belief in, and worship of the Christian religion's Devil is not even embraced by true Satanists who follow the teachings of the late Anton Szandor LaVey, who was an atheist.

However, in the old practice of Christian folk magick during the Middle Ages, the Devil figured prominently. Many of the spells and amulets used by the Christian Church and its faithful during that period were designed to keep their Devil at bay, and many of the dark superstitions that haunted the daily lives of the God-fearing had to do, in one way or another, with the Devil.

Can a Christian be a spellcrafter?

Christians are, and have always been, spellcrafters—whether or not they realize it or dare to admit it to themselves or to the world. (Of course, this is not the same thing as being a Witch, a Wiccan, or a Pagan.)

The recitations of prayers (which are basically verbal incantations) might very well be called the Christian version of casting spells. The Christian's religious symbol of the cross (which, incidentally, was a Pagan religious and magickal symbol throughout pre-Christian Europe and western Asia) is worn and displayed for protection against evil, which makes it no less of an amulet now than it was before the Christians claimed it as their own. Other popular Christian amulets include Saint Christopher medals, Saint Joseph statues, and scraps of the scriptural texts.

In addition, many of the saints invoked by Christians were originally Pagan deities and oracles who were canonized after their shrines were taken over by the Church. Most of the Christian holidays (such as Christmas, Easter, All Souls' Day, and Candlemas) were originally Pagan fertility festivals before being Christianized, and many of the rituals and customs associated with the religion of Christianity are deeply rooted in European Paganism.

In the Middle Ages, despite the Church's condemnation of the magickal arts as a device of the Devil, it was very common for good Christian folk to work spells and charms in the name of Jesus Christ, Mother Mary, or God. Numerous magickal workings and divinations have long been associated with the Bible and holy water, and psalms and masses were often used as verbal charms for protection, fertility, exorcism, healing, and controlling the forces of nature. Historically, Christians appear to have worked as much magick—if not more—than those who practiced Witchcraft.

In *The Woman's Encyclopedia of Myths and Secrets,* Barbara Walker sums up the Christian belief in miracles with the observation that "magick" and "miracles" were but different words for the same idea.

Can a Christian be a spellcrafter? Perhaps the answer lies in the humor of the Pagan bumper sticker that reads:

Christians Make the Best Voodoo Practitioners

Do Witches recite the Lord's Prayer backwards?

Throughout Europe in the Middle Ages, it was believed that Witches in attendance of Black Masses recited the Lord's Prayer in reverse to both evoke and pay homage to the Devil. The so-called Black Mass (which is believed by many occult historians to have been fabricated largely by judges of the Inquisition during the 14th and 15th centuries) was nothing more than a perversion of the Mass of the Christian liturgy (which, in turn, was a perversion of the ancient rites of the Pagan earth religions).

In his classic book, *Mastering Witchcraft,* author Paul Huson suggests that newcomers to the domain of Witchcraft perform "the time-honored tradition" of the backwards recitation of the Lord's Prayer as a symbolic gesture to "ceremonially demonstrate your severance from old restraints and inhibitions that in the past have acted as the main obstacles to the development of powers within you." The rite, which is referred to as "a process of blessed unbinding," should be performed by the light of a candle just before retiring, and repeated for three nights in a row. At the end of each prayer recitation, the phrase "So mote it be!" should be uttered and then the candle's flame extinguished.

Regardless of one's prior religion, the "defiant relic from the days of the great Witch persecutions" serves as "a process of purgation and catharsis" to liberate the new Witch from all inherited guilts and mark his or her first step on the Pagan path, according to Huson. However, this rite may only be effective to those who are renouncing Christianity, as the Lord's Prayer belongs to that religion.

The backwards recitation of the Lord's Prayer is not requisite to becoming a Witch or a spellcrafter, nor is it a ritual embraced by any known tradition of Wicca. However, if it is instrumental in helping you break free from the invisible shackles of Christianity and all of its "shalt's" and "shalt not's," then you should not hesitate to utilize it. Free thyself—mind, spirit, and soul—and blessed be!

What is a power hand?

Many psychics, diviners, spiritual healers, and practitioners of the magickal arts believe that certain energies (such as magickal, healing, and psychic) can be transmitted, as well as received through human hands. Of a person's two hands, one is said to naturally possess more power to transmit energy, while the other possesses more receptive power. The hand that is used to transmit is called the power hand. The right hand is the power hand for most people who are naturally right-handed, and the opposite applies to those who are naturally left-handed.

The mysterious powers of the hand have been used to heal and bless, as well as to curse, since the earliest recorded history. The index finger of a Witch's power hand has long been regarded by some as a part of the body containing the greatest magickal power, and in Medieval times, many Christians believed that a Witch could bring death simply by pointing her index finger at her intended victim.

Certain hand gestures made with one's power hands have been employed by various cultures throughout the world as charms to avert the evil eye, keep the Devil at bay, promote fertility, invoke deities, lay curses, and so forth.

What is meant by "high" and "low" magick?

High magick, also known as "true magick," is a term that refers to the type of ritual work performed by practitioners of ceremonial magick. High magick typically involves ancient grimiores, elaborate and complicated rituals, the use of planetary talismans, and the evocation of angels, demons, and ancient gods. Much of high magick is Judeo-Christian in its nature and origin, and several examples would be Kaballah, Goetia, Thelema, Enochian, Gnosticism, and Abramelin magick.

Low magick, on the other hand, refers to the more simplistic, Earth-oriented magick characteristic of Witches, Wiccans, Neo-Pagans, Druids, Shamans, Medicine Men and Women, Pow-Wowers, folk healers, and witch doctors. Sympathetic and imitative magick, herbal enchantment, charms and fetishes, candle magick, love magick, potion-brewing, mojo magick, hexcraft, and Hoodoo folk magick are but several examples of what many regard as low magick.

What is the Threefold Law, and how does it relate to spellcrafting?

The Threefold Law is also known as the Law of Three. It derives from the Hindu concept of karma and was incorporated into the Gardnerian tradition of Wicca by its founder, Gerald Gardner, who developed an interest in Oriental spiritual beliefs while working for the British government as an opium inspector in the Far East. Prior to the writings of Gardner in the mid-20th century, the concept of karma (threefold or otherwise) had never existed in the practice of Witchcraft in any part of the world.

The Threefold Law appears to be unique to Wicca and some Neo-Pagan circles. It holds that all human actions—whether good or evil—are returned three times or in tripled intensity by the mysterious "Lords of Karma," who preside over the law of cause and effect. Many Wiccans view the Threefold Law as a significant incentive not to practice black magick or cast spells that manipulate the free will of others.

The problems with the Threefold Law are that it defies the known laws of the universe and is felt by many non-Wiccans to be "out of balance." It manipulates the free will of those who believe in it by inducing paranoia and imposing fear of retribution and punishment, and it presupposes that magick (which is simply a form of energy, not unlike electricity) can somehow differentiate between what is "good" and what is "bad"—according to society's views. I have also seen many Wiccans become frighteningly overzealous where the Threefold Law and the Wiccan Rede are concerned, ranting and raving about them in much the same manner that fanatical born-again Christians carry on about the wrath of God and the Ten Commandments.

I am one Witch who does not embrace the Wiccan concept of the Threefold Law. I personally refuse to enslave my mind to, and allow my life to be plagued by, a law written by an author to fit in with his own personal beliefs. In my opinion, if you psychically set yourself up to believe that you will receive a threefold punishment as a result of your spellwork, as so many Wiccans have been taught to do, then chances are that this is exactly what you will get! It's the same if a healthy person convinces himself that he is sick or dying. Sooner or later his body will respond to his negative thought energies and begin to show signs of illness. Pain may be felt, an actual disease may manifest, and the victim of his own fears may even die as a result of what he had physically set himself up to believe.

Those are my personal thoughts on the Threefold Law. Some Wiccans will agree with my views, and some will undoubtedly disagree, which is their prerogative. But one thing I'm confident most people in the Craft will agree upon is that not all of us in the magickal community subscribe to the same set of practices, beliefs, and principles associated with the Wiccan religion. And certainly one's ethics, like the concept of "good" and "bad," are highly subjective. But it is this very diversity in magick and spirituality that makes the Pagan path a unique and beautiful thing.

Outside of the Wiccan traditions and a few Neo-Pagan circles that put their faith in the Threefold Law, those who practice the Old Religion of Witchcraft (which is a path far more old and diverse than Wicca and it's mid-20th century roots), do not feel a need to be policed by a Threefold Law or Lords of Karma. Most Witches acknowledge what is known as an "energy return" (which is not threefold, karmic, or retributional) and nearly all believe that a Witch should only do what a Witch feels in his or her heart is the right thing, and to always allow others to decide for themselves what is right and what is wrong. Love is the law.

Chapter 2

Magickal Correspondences

I n the art of spellcraft, correspondences are things, times, and symbols that share the same magickal energies and vibrations. They help Witches to focus on their desires and thus greatly enhance the power of spells. The use of magickal correspondences is probably as old as the practice of the magickal arts itself, and it is said that the more correspondences you incorporate into your spellwork, the greater your chances for obtaining successful magickal results are.

For instance, if you were to use correspondences in a spell to bring more money into your life, you would perform the spell during a waxing moon (the time of increase), use a new green candle, invoke a deity associated with prosperity, burn a money-attracting incense (such as pine), brew a potion from herbs that possess the correct magickal properties for money spells, and so forth.

You should keep in mind, however, that although correspondences may be beneficial tools for magickal workings, they are merely tools and are not the magick themselves. The real magick, of course, comes from your heart! For truly successful magick, you must combine the correspondences you use with creative visualization and the power of your own will. If you are new to spellcasting, it may take a bit of practice before you are able to master this, so don't become discouraged and give up if you do not achieve immediate results.

Color Correspondences

Color correspondences are an essential aspect of candle magick, as each color possesses a unique vibration, attribute, symbolism, and influence. Therefore, it is important to work only with candle colors that match your magickal intents.

Black: Some people associate black candles only with the left-hand path; however, black is a color that actually banishes negativity and evil influences. Ideal for breaking hexes, jinxes, and curses. One of the traditional colors of the Samhain Sabbat and the Goddess in Her Crone aspect.

Blue: The color of peace and tranquility, baby boys, spiritual awareness, and protection during sleep; the astrological signs of Aquarius, Pisces, and Virgo; and the throat chakra (royal blue).

Brown: Spells involving the protection of familiars and household pets, locating lost objects, and the solving of problems concerning the home; possesses potent and beneficial energy vibrations for people born under the astrological sign of Capricorn.

Gold: The sacred color of all solar deities; spells involving intuition and protection; the astrological sign of Leo; the heart chakra.

Gray: Used in candle magick primarily for the neutralizing of negative energies; the astrological sign of Virgo. Some spellcasters use gray candles in the practice of what is known as "gray magick."

Green: Spells involving fertility, healing, luck, money, and prosperity; rituals to counteract greed and jealousy; the astrological sign of Capricorn; the solar plexus chakra; a color sacred to all fertility deities.

Orange: Spells involving courage, legal matters, concentration, and encouragement; the root chakra; one of the colors associated with the sign of Taurus and the Sabbat of Samhain.

Pink: Spells involving love (both sexual and platonic), baby girls, femininity, friendships, and the overcoming of evil; the astrological sign of Taurus (mauve).

Purple: All things of a psychic nature, divination, independence, and ambition; the astrological signs of Libra and Sagittarius; the crown chakra.

Red: Spells involving love, magnetism, passion, physical health, sexuality, strength, and willpower; the astrological signs of Aries and Scorpio; the sacral chakra; all gods and goddesses of love.

Silver: Associated with moon-magick and all lunar deities; the astrological sign of Cancer.

Yellow: Spells involving confidence, persuasion, school, and the mental powers; the astrological sign of Gemini; the brow (or third eye) chakra.

White: The sacred color of the Goddess. Use white candles for exorcism, meditation, purification, and spells involving spirituality, truth, virginity, and new beginnings.

Calendar Correspondences

The seven days of the week and the eight Sabbats of the Wheel of the Year also correspond to various candle colors, among other things:

Sunday: Yellow, the Sun, all solar deities, magick that concerns authority, divine power, friendships, healing, learning, reason, and world leaders.

Monday: White, the Moon, all lunar deities, magick that concerns cooking, dreams, family, the home, intuition, medicine, spiritual growth, and the ocean.

Tuesday: Red, the planet Mars, the god Tiw, magick that concerns athletics, competitions, conflicts, courage, hunting, legality, logic, physical strength, politics, vitality, and war.

Wednesday: Purple, the planet Mercury, the god Woden, magick that concerns communication, divination, education, mystical insight, predictions, resourcefulness, and self-improvement.

Thursday: Blue, the planet Jupiter, the god Thor, magick that concerns dedication, endurance, faithfulness, legal matters, loyalty, luck, and money matters.

Friday: Green, the planet Venus, the goddess Frigg, magick that concerns art, fertility, love, music, partnerships, and pleasure.

Saturday: Black, the planet and god Saturn, magick that concerns banishing, change, death, motivation, reincarnation, understanding, and wills.

Oimelc/Candlemas (February 2): White.

Spring Equinox (First day of Spring): All colors of the rainbow, Aries/Fire.

Beltane/Walpurgisnacht (May 1): Dark green.

Summer Solstice (First day of Summer): Green and blue, Cancer/Water.

Lughnasadh/Lammas (August 1): Gold and all harvest colors.

Autumn Equinox (First day of Autumn): Brown, orange, and yellow, Libra/Air.

Samhain (October 31): Black and orange.

Winter Solstice (First day of Winter): Gold, green, red, and silver, Capricorn/Earth.

Lunar Correspondences

The Waxing Moon is the correct lunar phase during which to perform all types of magick for healing, attracting good luck, and increasing things (such as money and love). It traditionally corresponds to the Goddess in Her aspect of the Maiden (also known as the Virgin or Warrioress); the season of Spring; the colors green and red; the goddess Diana (Artemis); the physical; the Earth; and growth and sensuality.

The Full Moon (which symbolizes the pregnant Mother Goddess) corresponds to the season of Summer; the colors silver and white; the ancient goddess Selene (Luna); the emotional and psychic; the sky; the cauldron; and motherhood and creation. The powers of various magickal practices are said to be at their greatest when the night is illuminated by the light of the full moon. Fertility rites, divinations, and problem-solving magick are but a few examples of spellwork that is often performed during this lunar phase.

The Waning Moon traditionally corresponds to the Goddess in Her aspect of the Crone; the seasons of Fall and Winter; the colors gray and black; the ancient goddess Hecate; the spiritual; the underworld; death and transformation. When the moon is in its waning phase, the time is right for all forms of spellwork that involve banishing, binding, and eliminating things (such as negativity, bad habits, disease, obstacles, and so forth).

Astrological Correspondences

Aries: The Element of Fire; yang energy; positive polarity; the planet Mars; the head; Tuesday; the numbers one and nine; diamond; the color red; all thorn-bearing trees; iron; sheep, and rams.

Taurus: The Element of Earth; yin energy; negative polarity; the planet Venus; the neck and throat; Friday; the numbers four and six; emerald; the colors light blue and mauve; cypress and apple trees; copper; and cattle (especially bulls).

Gemeni: The Element of Air; yang energy; positive polarity; the planet Mercury; the hands, arms, shoulders and lungs; Wednesday; the numbers five and nine; agate, the color yellow; all nut-bearing trees; mercury; butterflies; and brightly colored birds.

Cancer: The Element of Water; yin energy; negative polarity; the Moon; the breasts and stomach, Monday; the numbers three and seven; pearl; the colors sea green and silver; trees rich in sap; the metal silver; crabs, and animals with shell coverings.

Leo: The Element of Fire; yang energy; positive polarity; the Sun; the back, spine, and heart, Sunday; the numbers eight and nine; ruby; the colors gold and orange; all citrus trees; the metal gold; and all felines (particularly lions).

Virgo: The Element of Earth; yin energy; negative polarity; the planet Mercury; the nervous system and the intestines, Wednesday; the numbers three and five; sapphire; the colors gray and navy blue; all nut-bearing trees; quicksilver; and small household pets.

Libra: The Element of Air; yang energy; positive polarity; the planet Venus; the lower back, buttocks, and kidneys; Friday; the numbers six and nine; opal; the colors blue and lavender; almond, ash, and cypress trees; and copper snakes, and lizards.

Scorpio: The Element of Water; yin energy; negative polarity; the planet Mars; the sexual organs; Tuesday; the numbers two and four; topaz; all dark shades of red; blackthorn trees; plutonium; scorpions, and insects.

Sagittarius: The Element of Fire; yang energy; positive polarity; the planet Jupiter; the liver, hips, and thighs, Thursday; the numbers five and seven; turquoise; the color purple; birch, mulberry, and oak trees; tin; and horses, centaurs, and unicorns.

Capricorn: The Element of Earth; yin energy; negative polarity; the planet Saturn; the bones; knees, teeth, and skin; Saturday; the numbers two and eight; garnet; the colors brown and dark green; elm, pine, and poplar trees; lead; goats, and all animals with cloven hoofs.

Aquarius: The Element of Air; yang energy; positive polarity; the planet Uranus; the blood, calves, shins, and ankles; Wednesday; the numbers one and seven; amethyst; the color blue; all fruit trees; uranium, and birds.

Pieces: The Element of Water; yin energy; negative polarity; the planet Neptune; the feet and lymph glands; Friday; the numbers two and six; the colors aquamarine and pale green; fig and willow trees; platinum, and fish.

Chapter 3

A Time for Magick

Working in harmony with lunar phases, moon signs, seasonal transitions, Sabbats, and the planetary hours is of the utmost importance in the art of spellcrafting and one of the keys to success in magick. Timing is everything for a Witch or a magician, for a spell that is timed just right will have a far better chance of hitting its mark than one that is not. This is an important rule to always bear in mind—especially when designing your own personal spells from scratch.

In his book *Gypsy Witchcraft and Magic*, Raymond Buckland states that magick should never be rushed, and adds, "Most magic needs to be done at the right time, whether by the hour of the day or night, or by the time of the month, so plan ahead for it." He further advises against working magick "on the spur of the moment," for this rarely brings success.

Lunar Magick

"A great part of genuine witchcraft is moon magic, derived from the age-old lore of moon worship."

—Doreen Valiente, *An ABC of Witchcraft Past and Present*

New Moon

Spellcraft that pertains to beginnings is best carried out when the moon is new. This is the appropriate lunar phase during which to create magickal tools, start a new project, and cast spells and perform rituals involving such things as birth, virginity, new ideas, wish-magick, the hunt, and bringing something into being.

The turning of silver coins in one's pocket to increase wealth is an old act of magick traditionally performed during a new moon. The first new moon of the year is believed by some to induce prophetic dreams (especially of one's future marriage partner) when a special incantation, such as the following, is thrice recited:

> *All hail, new moon, all hail to thee!*
> *I prithee, good moon, reveal to me,*
> *This night who shall my true love be.*

According to ancient occult tradition of England, the third day immediately following a new moon is "an inauspicious day for most undertakings." Also, beware of new moons that fall on Saturdays or Sundays, for these are said to be followed by bad luck and foul weather. Old lunar lore from Pagan Britain states that pointing a finger at the new moon invites bad luck into your life. Interestingly, this belief eventually found its way into the realm of Christian superstition, where it held that pointing at the moon nine times kept a person from ever going to heaven. It is doubtful that the number nine was chosen for this superstition by mere chance, as it has always been regarded as the most magickal of all numbers by Witches, magicians, and those who dabble in the occult.

*An ancient lunar goddess holds a crescent moon
in her right hand.*

Waxing Moon

Spellcraft that increases or attracts is best carried out when
the moon is waxing. This is the appropriate lunar phase during
which to cast spells and perform rituals involving such things as
birth, strength, growth, planting gardens, friendships, harmony,
happiness, obtaining things and goals, travel, protection, teaching, weather-working (to bring forth), and positive change. Love
magick and spells for health, good luck, and money are traditionally performed during a waxing moon.

In the Goddess-oriented tradition of Wicca, this lunar phase
corresponds to the Maiden (also Warrioress and Virgin) aspect
of the Triple Goddess.

Full Moon

The full moon is said to be the phase when lunar energies
are at their peak, and it is also the traditional time of the month
when Witches' covens have their monthly meetings, known as
esbats. Additionally, most Witches' psychic powers are at their
greatest when the moon is full.

Spellcraft that energizes, empowers, illuminates, transforms, and fulfills is best carried out when the moon is full. This is the appropriate lunar phase during which to cast spells and perform rituals involving such things as fertility, virility, creativity, beauty, health, blessings, communication, divination, happiness, intuition, shapeshifting, spirit conjurations, teaching, unions, wish-magick, nurturing love-magick, passion, sexuality, dreamwork (especially to facilitate prophetic dreams), and anything of a psychic nature.

> *Pray to the Moon when she is round.*
> *Luck with you will then abound.*
> *What you seek for shall be found,*
> *On the sea or solid ground.*
>
> —An old Pagan rhyme (origin unknown)

A full moon is said to cause madness in men, and the old saying, "when the Moon's in the full, then wit's in the wane" clearly reflects this. In parts of Europe where belief in lycanthropy was once common among royalty and peasantry alike, the full moon was greatly feared, for its very essence activated the animal transformations in men afflicted with the curse of a werewolf.

Wart-curing spells have been performed when the moon is full probably since magick was first practiced. Witches in northern England were said to have been able to magickally remove any wart from any part of the body simply by blowing their breath upon it in the light of the full moon. "Washing" one's hands in a well-polished silver basin, filled only with the rays of the full moon, while reciting a magickal incantation was another method once used by Witches and folk healers to eliminate warts from the fingers and hands.

In the Goddess-oriented tradition of Wicca, the full moon corresponds to the Mother aspect of the Triple Goddess, making it the appropriate time for Mother Goddess invocations and all spells and ritual work pertaining to motherhood.

Waning Moon

Spellcraft that decreases, banishes, or brings things to an end is best carried out when the moon is waning. This is the appropriate lunar phase during which to cast spells and perform rituals involving such things as release, reversal, death and resurrection, healing, wisdom, maturity, counter-magick, liberation, overcoming, weather-working (to quell), weight loss, real estate (to sell), and the breaking of addictions, bad habits, and streaks of bad luck.

Banishings, bindings, exorcisms, and both the casting and breaking of curses are also traditionally performed during the waning moon.

In the Goddess-oriented traditions of Wicca, this lunar phase corresponds to the Crone aspect of the Triple Goddess, and many Wiccans (especially those who are post-menopausal women) perform Crone (or Dark Goddess) honoring rites when the moon is on the wane.

The Dark Moon

The dark moon is the three-and-a-half-day period just before the moon is new. The moon is not visible in the sky during this time, and those who practice spellcraft in accordance with the energies of the lunar phases refrain from all magickal activity until the time of the dark moon passes. According to ancient moon lore, any spells cast during the dark moon are unlikely to bring forth the results one desires.

Most modern Witches observe the dark moon as a time of rest and recuperation. It is an ideal time for meditation, vision questing, and the planning of future spellwork.

Void-of-course Moon

A void-of-course moon occurs every two to three days and refers to the time between the moon's final aspect in any sign of the zodiac and the moment it enters the next one. This can range in time from several minutes to several hours.

Traditionally, when the moon is void-of-course, spellwork is given a rest. Many astrologically minded Witches believe that spells cast during this time are greatly prone to failure; however, meditation is enhanced during this time, and many folks find that it is a favorable time for performing divinations and working with dreams. In reference to a void-of-course moon, author Nicholas de Yore states in the *Encyclopedia of Astrology* that, "When the Moon is so placed it denies fruition to much of the good otherwise promised in the Figure."

Eclipses

Since ancient times, eclipses (both lunar and solar) have been regarded by many cultures as the bringers of storms, earthquakes, and other furies of Mother Nature, ill luck, bad omens, and even the wrath of the gods. Historically, eclipses have presaged the deaths and assassinations of many high-ranking political figures (such as the Roman Emperor Nero and Catherine of Aragon, the first wife of England's King Henry VIII), plagues (such as the Black Death in 1348), and wars (such as World War I in 1914). It is not difficult to see why eclipses have long filled people throughout the world with a sense of dread and have earned such an ominous reputation.

Medieval lore and many ancient grimoires warn against the casting of spells or the performing of any magickal rites on the day or night that an eclipse occurs. Most modern-day spellcrafters continue to heed the advice of the ancients—not because they fear being struck down from a lightning bolt hurled by some angry god, but instead because during an eclipse the lunar or solar lines of force are severed, and this results in one's magick being nullified.

There are some Pagans who regard an eclipse to be magickally significant and perform rituals during them to draw upon their power. I personally do not see any harm in such a thing, but I for one would never waste my time and energy attempting to carry out magickal workings during an eclipse. But to each his own, as the old saying goes.

Elemental Spells

Earth spells are best performed when the moon is positioned in one of the three astrological signs ruled by the Element of Earth: Taurus, Virgo, and Capricorn. Examples of Earth spells include invocations of Earth Elementals, rituals involving persons born under an Earth sign, and spells involving such things as animals, career, employment, fertility, healing, herbs, money, and prosperity.

Air spells are best performed when the moon is positioned in one of the three astrological signs ruled by the Element of Air: Aquarius, Gemini, and Libra. Examples of Air spells include invocations of Air Elementals, rituals involving persons born under an Air sign, and spells involving such things as communication, mental powers, psychic abilities, visions, and wisdom.

Fire spells are best performed when the moon is positioned in one of the three astrological signs ruled by the Element of Fire: Aries, Leo, and Sagittarius. Examples of Fire spells include invocations of Fire Elementals, rituals involving persons born under a Fire sign, and spells involving such things as courage, exorcism of demons and ghosts, health, lust, protection, revenge, and strength.

Water spells are best performed when the moon is positioned in one of the three astrological signs ruled by the Element of Water: Pisces, Cancer, and Scorpio. Examples of Water spells include invocations of Water Elementals, rituals involving persons born under a Water sign, and spells involving such things as dreams (especially those of a prophetic nature), friendships, healing (both on a physical and emotional level), love, meditation, purification, and sleep.

The Witching Hour

Midnight is said to be the time when the restless spirits of the dead rise up out of their graves, strange and terrifying creatures of the supernatural walk the earth, and the shadows of the occult grow their darkest and most powerful. But is there any truth behind such beliefs, or are they merely myths that have managed to survive the passing of the centuries?

The hour of midnight has long been known as the "witching hour," for this is when the clairvoyant and spellcasting powers of all Witches and sorcerers are believed to be at their peak. It is a special time of magick and transformation, as well as of romance and mystery. When Lady Luna is full and shining brightly, midnight becomes a witching hour of the greatest power, and it is the traditional time of the month for rituals known as Drawing Down the Moon to be held. The witching hour is also the traditional time for esbats to begin. However, some covens prefer to hold their esbats at the New Moon. It is a time when religious worship is conducted, business matters relating to the coven are discussed, and healings and magickal spells are carried out. In most traditions of the Craft, a Cakes and Wine ritual normally follows an esbat.

In ancient times, the power of the witching hour was applied not only to the casting of spells, curses, and bindings, but also to divination, necromancy, spirit conjurations, shapeshifting, certain alchemical workings, the crafting of magickal talismans and amulets, the constructing of ritual tools, and other purposes.

Traditionally, the witching hour on a night of the waxing moon is the correct time for the casting of spells, the brewing of potions, and the working of charms to increase one's wealth, strengthen the physical body, attract good luck, inspire love and lust, and tune into psychic abilities.

During the dark period in human history dominated by the bloodlust of the Inquisition, it was widely believed that sorcerers and sorceresses alike practiced their black arts when the witching hour was accompanied by a waning moon. Curses, hexes, and other forms of maleficia would be cast upon enemies to bring them bad luck and ruin. In some cases, according to an old book on Witchcraft and demonology, midnight sorcery was used to deliver illness, insanity, and even death!

However, most contemporary Witches and Pagans work with the power of the waning moon to energize spells, potions, and charms that are designed for curing illnesses, banishing negativity and all manners of evil, binding those who do harm, lifting curses, breaking hexes, and reversing love spells. A witching hour in the dark phase of the Moon is regarded by some occultists to be a dangerous time to work magick; it is associated with the ancient Pagan gods and goddesses of the underworld and the conjuration of all things evil. Many contemporary practitioners of the Craft avoid working magick at this time of the month.

The witching hour is believed to have been named as such back in medieval times. However, the association between Witches and the midnight hour/phase of the Moon dates back to early times, when magick and the worship of female lunar deities who presided over fertility was widespread throughout Europe and other parts of the world.

The "veil between the worlds" is believed to be most thin at midnight, which explains why encounters with ghosts, Fairy-folk, and other supernaturals occur most often during this time of night. The witching hour of midnight is not only a very magickal time, but one surrounded by centuries of folklore, superstitious beliefs, and omens as well. These include the following:

- ⊗ If a clock strikes 13 times instead of 12 at the hour of midnight, it is regarded as a bad omen. Another version of this superstition holds that the 13th chime conjures up the Devil.

- ⊗ In England, it is said that dire misfortune will find its way into the lives of the royal family within three months if London's Big Ben strikes irregularly at the midnight hour.

- ⊗ According to ancient legend, Witches can make themselves invisible or turn into animals when the clock strikes 12. The witching hour is also said to be the time when all spells, whether they be of black or white magick, take effect.

✸ The witching hour can bring on a temporary fit of insanity known as "midnight madness" in certain individuals. This often ties in with the full moon and its reputed power to produce lunacy (or "moon madness") and, in some cases, zoomorphism—especially lycanthropy.

✸ Midnight is the transformational point when one day turns into the next. In the minds of the ancients, this unequivocally linked the witching hour not only to the transformation of time, but to physical transformation (shapeshifting) as well.

✸ In old European folklore, the midnight hour—especially when the Moon is full—is the time when rampages awaken from their dreamless slumber, ghouls roam the graveyards, demons manifest, and cursed men transform into werewolves to prowl the earth in search of human victims. It is not until the first rays of dawn's golden light illuminate the horizon that the living are truly safe from the evil of these supernatural monstrosities.

✸ Seances are traditionally held at midnight, for most spiritualist mediums believe it is at this time, when the post meridian and ante meridian intersect, that the spirits of the dead grow restless and communication with the spirit world is best achieved. According to the published research of numerous paranormal investigators, the witching hour seems to be the prime time for most hauntings and poltergeist activity to occur.

✸ The midnight hour of Halloween (the Witches' Sabbat of Samhain) is a very special time. For centuries, this has been the traditional time for unmarried ladies and gents to perform annual rituals of love divination to determine who their future spouses will be and what they will be like. Although most Halloween midnight divinations are concerned with matters of an amatory nature, a number of divinatory methods exist in Ireland and parts of Great Britain that are used for determining whether a certain person will live to see the next Halloween.

✦ Midnight on the 31st of October is also a time surrounded by a vast number of folk beliefs and superstitions. For instance, if you should hear footsteps following closely behind you at midnight on Halloween, take care not to turn around and look because it may be the Grim Reaper (or, in some versions, the Devil) coming to claim you. If a person casts no shadow at midnight on Halloween, this is said to be an omen of his or her death. Another old superstition holds that the apparitions of all persons destined to die before the next Halloween can be observed walking through, or floating above, churchyards at the witching hour on All Hallows' Eve.

The energies of the witching hour enhance all forms of magick, meditation, and divination, which is beneficial to all Witches and Pagans, regardless of their tradition. So the next time you hear the tolling of the midnight bells, allow the "hour of power" to cast its spell upon you.

There is no other time of the day or night that comes close to being as magickal, mystical, and mysterious as the one known as the witching hour.

Seasonal Transitions, Sabbats, and Other Magickal Days

January 1

The first day of the year is traditionally observed by many Witches throughout the world with the casting of a spell to ensure good luck throughout the coming year. New Year's Day is also an ideal time for working magick involving personal resolutions and rituals to bless the new year with peace, love, good health, and prosperity for all. (Spells for the new year can be found in Chapter 7.)

January 21

Saint Agnes' Day is a time of the year associated with the brewing of love philtres (potions) and the casting of love enchantments. Divinations to make a vision of one's future husband appear in a dream have been traditionally performed on Saint Agnes' Eve (January 20) for centuries.

To dream of the man or woman who shall be your future spouse, it is said that you must spend the entire day of the eve of Saint Agnes in fasting and complete silence, eating only a bit of stale bread and drinking tea brewed from parsley. At bedtime, remove your shoes and put a sprig of rosemary into one and a sprig of thyme into the other. Place one shoe at each side of your bed's headboard and then thrice recite the following incantation:

> *Herb of rosemary,*
> *Herb of thyme,*
> *I enchant thee by this rhyme.*
> *Before Saint Agnes' Eve is done*
> *Let me dream about the one*
> *Destined to be my love so true,*
> *Let his (her) face come into view!*
> *So mote it be.*

February 2

Candlemas (also known as Imbolc and Oimelc) is a Fire festival and, in certain traditions of Wicca, a Sabbat dedicated to the goddess Brigid. The types of spellcasting traditionally associated with this time of year include, but are not limited to, weather divination, personal power-raising rituals, spells that focus on new beginnings and spiritual growth, healings, protective magick, spells involving sacred groves and wells, candle blessings, candle scrying (gazing), and candle-burning rituals. (You'll find Candlemas spells in Chapter 7.)

February 14

Saint Valentine's Day is a time of the year when love energy abounds and amatory thoughts are on the minds of many ladies and gents. As with Saint Agnes' Day, this is a favorable time for the brewing of love philtres, the casting of love enchantments, the making or purchasing of love amulets, and the performing of rituals to divine one's future marriage mate. (See the Love-Drawing Bath in Chapter 7.)

March 21 (approximate date)

The Spring, or Vernal, Equinox (also called Ostara, after the name of a Saxon fertility goddess) is a time of the year when the hours of day and night are equal. The types of spellcasting traditionally associated with the Spring Equinox include, but are not limited to, fertility rites, the working of spells and rituals to restore balance in one's life, gardening spells, seed-blessing rituals, and oomantia (the ancient art and practice of divination by eggs). To magickally induce a dream that reveals the identity of your future marriage partner, place a hen's egg under your pillow before going to bed on the eve of the Spring Equinox. Some traditions specify that "the first egg laid by a white pullet" must be used in order for the spell to work.

To divine your future spouse's occupation, an old Gypsy method calls for the white of a newly-laid egg from a white hen to be poured into a glass of water, which is left to stand for five minutes upon a sunny window sill. After this time, the symbolic shapes that the egg whites assume as they rise to the surface of the water can be interpreted. For instance, if the shape of a ship is seen, this may indicate that your future spouse will be a seaman or a fisherman; a shoe may symbolize the profession of a cobbler; a book may indicate a teacher, writer, or librarian; and so forth. If a death symbol, such as a skull or a coffin, is formed by the egg whites, this may indicate the profession of an undertaker. However, in some instances it can be an unlucky omen portending widowhood.

May 1

Beltane (also known as May Day and Walpurgisnacht) falls opposite Samhain on the Wheel of the Year and is a Sabbat rooted in an ancient Celtic fire festival. The types of spellcasting traditionally associated with this time of year include, but are not limited to, fertility rites, sex-magic, fairy blessings and enchantments, healings, spellwork involving animals, ritual purification, and protective magick. (Beltane spells can be found in Chapter 7.)

June 21 (approximate date)

The Summer Solstice (also known as Midsummer, Litha, Saint John's Day, and many other names) marks the longest day and shortest night of the year. At sunrise on this day, many Witches around the world continue to carry on the old Pagan tradition of gathering magickal and medicinal herbs from gardens or from the wild to use in potions, dream pillows, poppets, and so forth. The types of spellcasting traditionally associated with this time of the year include, but are not limited to, fertility/virility rites, protective magick (especially the crafting of amulets for protection), animal blessings, vision questing, divinations (particularly through dreams and visions), and rituals involving abundance, empowerment, consummation, or culmination.

August 1

Lammas (also known as Lughnasadh) is the first of the three harvest Sabbats. In certain traditions of Wicca it is dedicated to the ancient Celtic solar deity, Lugh, or to the Great Goddess of the Grain (such as Demeter, Ceres, and Ops.) Lammas is also known as the Feast of Bread. The types of spellcasting traditionally associated with this time of year include, but are not limited to, thanksgiving rituals, harvest spells, fertility rites, corn dolly spells, spells and divinations involving bread, and Pagan rites involving death and resurrection. (Several Lammas spells appear in Chapter 7.)

August 13

This day is sacred to the Greek deity Hecate (a goddess of both the moon and of crossroads, known since the Middle Ages as the "Queen of Witches"), and her festival has been celebrated by Pagans on this date for many centuries. The types of spellcasting traditionally associated with this time of the year include, but are not limited to, spells and rituals involving magickal empowerment, journeys, prophecy, fertility, protection, dark magick, and spirits of the dead. Hecate invocations, an example of which can be found in my book *Wicca Craft*, are traditionally held during the witching hour at places where three roads meet.

September 21 (approximate date)

The Fall, or Autumnal, Equinox (also called Mabon, after the Welsh god of fertility) is the second of the three Harvest Sabbats, the Witches' Thanksgiving, and a time of the year when the hours of the day and night are equal. The types of spellcasting traditionally associated with this time of the year include, but are not limited to, thanksgiving rituals, vision questing, harvest rites, divination, and the working of spells and rituals to restore balance in one's life.

October 31

Samhain (also known as Halloween, All Hallow's Eve, Shadowfest, and many other names) is a major Sabbat that marks both the end and the beginning of the Wheel of the Year. It is said to be the time when the veil that stands between the world of the living and the world of the dead is at its thinnest. It is the final Harvest Sabbat, and the most sacred and magickal night of the year to Witches in many parts of the world. Sadly, some unenlightened individuals are under the impression that Samhain is a time for curses and hexes to be cast and for all manners of Satanic rites to be performed, but nothing could be further from the truth! The types of spellcasting traditionally associated with this time of the year include, but are not limited to, harvest rites, divinations (especially those involving affairs of the heart, matrimony, and death), scrying, protective magick, rites to honor the dead and to make contact with spirits, exorcism, banishings, bindings, and uncrossing rituals.

Spell to enchant a crystal ball

Before crystal-gazing on Samhain night, perform the following enchantment to obtain more favorable results from your scrying. Place a yellow candle at each side of your crystal ball, and place mugwort around the base of the ball or beneath it. Light the wicks of the candles with a match, place your power hand upon the top of the crystal ball, and then recite the following chant repeatedly until you feel the crystal ball tingling with power:

> *Visions of the future,*
> *And visions of the old,*
> *Through this ball of crystal*
> *Let my eyes behold.*

December 21 (approximate date)

The Winter Solstice (also known as Yule and Midwinter) marks the longest night and shortest day of the year. The types of spellcasting traditionally associated with this time of the year include, but are not limited to, spells and divinations involving Yule logs, Yule candles, and mistletoe, contact with spirits of the dead, spells for strength and health, wish-magick, and spells to attract good luck into one's life. (Refer to Chapter 11 for a variety of Yuletide spells, recipes, and superstitions.)

Planetary Hours

Since the dawn of history, mankind has developed numerous ways to measure time. One such method is known as planetary hours.

For practitioners of the magickal arts, timing is of the utmost importance, as most believe that there are magickal/psychic "tides" which, not unlike the tides of the ocean, ebb and flow at intervals. These tides exert a different energy or influence favorable to certain types of magick, especially where talismans are concerned. And in ceremonial magick it is believed that spirits (both angelic and demonic) possess affinities to certain days and times.

Planetary hours have been observed by magicians since ancient times, and their tables can be found in many old grimoires, such as the *Key of Solomon, The Clavicle, The Book of True Black Magick,* and others.

Planetary hours, according to Stewart Farrar in *What Witches Do*, "are the traditionally accepted hours for operating spells which have planetary correspondences." He further explains, "The first hour after sunrise is ruled by the day's own planet, after which each hour is ruled by one of the other planets in the order Sun, Venus, Mercury, Moon, Saturn, Jupiter, Mars, and so on in rotation."

Some spellcasters feel that it is not always necessary to incorporate the energies of the planetary hours into their spellcrafting. However, in cases where your energy level is reduced by illness or stress and a spell must still be performed, or if another person happens to be working against you on a magickal or psychic level, tapping into the energies of the planetary hours (along with those of the lunar phases) will add increased potency to a magickal working and bring you all the more closer to success.

To avoid confusion, be aware that there are also planetary hours connected to what is known as Medical Alchemy. These differ from the planetary hours used by practitioners of ceremonial magick and Witchcraft. In this astrologically based system of homeopathic healing, the seven planets (Sun, Moon, Mars, Mercury, Jupiter, Venus, Saturn) are divided into a 24-hour day, making each planetary hour approximately three hours and 25 minutes long. The planetary hours of Medical Alchemy do not pertain to the planetary hours listed in this chapter.

The first step to working your spellcraft in accordance with the planetary hours of magick is to understand that they are a different concept from time and are not the same hours that are determined each day by a clock. Each day of the week is made up of 24 planetary hours. The first 12 of these are considered day hours, and the following 12 are considered night hours. The first planetary hour of the day does not mean 1 a.m., nor does the 12th planetary hour of the night mean midnight. And unlike regular hours which are always made up of 60 minutes, a planetary hour, depending upon the season, may have more or less than 60 minutes at a time.

The first planetary hour of the day always begins at the precise hour and minute of sunrise. The first planetary hour of the night always begins at the precise hour and minute of sunset. To find out the exact times of sunrise and sunset, consult your local newspaper, a detailed calendar or almanac, the Weather Channel, or the Internet.

Calculating the planetary hours

Once you have determined when sunrise and sunset occur, the next step is to translate the time between these two points in the day into minutes, and then divide that number by 12. The resulting number will tell you how many minutes there are in each planetary hour of that day from sunrise to sunset. To figure out how many minutes are in the planetary hours of the night, add up the time in minutes between sunset and the next sunrise and then divide by 12. (See the example that follows.)

The first planetary hour of the day will begin at the exact time of sunrise and last for the number of minutes determined by the method of calculation just outlined. It will also correspond to the ruling planet of the day:

⊗   Sunday is ruled by the Sun.

⊗   Monday is ruled by the Moon.

⊗   Tuesday is ruled by Mars.

⊗   Wednesday is ruled by Mercury.

⊗   Thursday is ruled by Jupiter.

⊗   Friday is ruled by Venus.

⊗   Saturday is ruled by Saturn.

The second planetary hour of the day begins when the first one ends, the third begins when the second one ends, and so forth. Note that the dividing-line minute between two different planetary hours is known as a "cusp" (just like in astrology), and because of the unstable energy that occurs when two different planetary influences briefly come into contact with each other, this is not an ideal time for magickal workings to be undertaken.

Example

The following example will demonstrate how to figure out the planetary hours for a particular day:

If sunrise on a Sunday occurs at 5:57 a.m. and sunset occurs at 7:58 p.m., the period of time between these two points translates into 841 minutes, which is then divided by 12. The resulting number (which, in this case, is rounded to 70) indicates how many minutes are in each planetary hour of the day for Sunday. Thus, the first planetary hour of this particular day would begin at 5:57 a.m. (sunrise) and end 70 minutes later, at 7:07 a.m. This time period would also be ruled by the Sun, because the first planetary hour of each day corresponds to that day's ruling planet and Sunday happens to be ruled by the Sun.

The second planetary hour of the day (Venus) would begin at 7:07 a.m. and end 70 minutes later, at 8:17 a.m. The third planetary hour of the day (Mercury) would begin at 8:17 a.m. and end at 9:27 a.m., and so forth.

The Greater Key of Solomon

In the ancient grimoire known as *The Greater Key of Solomon,* the following information (through the end of this chapter) regarding the days and hours of each planet is given:

In the Days and Hours of Saturn, thou canst perform experiments to cause good or ill success to business, possessions, goods, seeds, fruit and similar things, in order to acquire learning; to bring destruction and give death, and to sow hatred and discord.

The Days and Hours of Jupiter are proper for obtaining honours, acquiring riches; contracting friendships, preserving health; and arriving at all that thou canst desire.

In the Days and Hours of Mars thou canst make experiments regarding war; to arrive at military honour; to acquire courage; to overthrow enemies; and further to cause ruin, slaughter, cruelty, discord; to wound and to give death.

The Days and Hours of the Sun are very good for perfecting experiments regarding temporal wealth, hope, gain, fortune, divination, the favour of princes, to dissolve hostile feeling, and to make friends.

The Days and Hours of Venus are good for forming friendships; for kindness and love; for joyous and pleasant undertakings, and for travelling.

The Days and Hours of Mercury are good to operate for eloquence and intelligence; promptitude in business; science and divination; wonders; apparitions; and answers regarding the future. Thou canst also operate under this Planet for thefts; writings; deceit; and merchandise.

The Days and Hours of the Moon are good for embassies; voyages; envoys; messages; navigation; reconciliation; love, and the acquisition of merchandise by water.

Note: For additional information, see the section on talismanic correspondences in the chapter called "Amulets, Talismans, Charms, and Fetishes."

The Planetary Hours of the Day
(sunrise to sunset)

Sunday

1. Sun	7. Mars
2. Venus	8. Sun
3. Mercury	9. Venus
4. Moon	10. Mercury
5. Saturn	11. Moon
6. Jupiter	12. Saturn

Monday

1. Moon	7. Mercury
2. Saturn	8. Moon
3. Jupiter	9. Saturn
4. Mars	10. Jupiter
5. Sun	11. Mars
6. Venus	12. Sun

Tuesday

1. Mars	7. Jupiter
2. Sun	8. Mars
3. Venus	9. Sun
4. Mercury	10. Venus
5. Moon	11. Mercury
6. Saturn	12. Moon

Wednesday

1. Mercury	7. Venus
2. Moon	8. Mercury
3. Saturn	9. Moon
4. Jupiter	10. Saturn
5. Mars	11. Jupiter
6. Sun	12. Mars

Thursday

1. Jupiter	7. Saturn
2. Mars	8. Jupiter
3. Sun	9. Mars
4. Venus	10. Sun
5. Mercury	11. Venus
6. Moon	12. Mercury

Friday

1. Venus	7. Sun
2. Mercury	8. Venus
3. Moon	9. Mercury
4. Saturn	10. Moon
5. Jupiter	11. Saturn
6. Mars	12. Jupiter

Saturday

1. Saturn	4. Sun	7. Moon	10. Mars
2. Jupiter	5. Venus	8. Saturn	11. Sun
3. Mars	6. Mercury	9. Jupiter	12. Venus

The Planetary Hours of the Night
(sunset to sunrise)

Sunday

1. Jupiter	7. Saturn
2. Mars	8. Jupiter
3. Sun	9. Mars
4. Venus	10. Sun
5. Mercury	11. Venus
6. Moon	12. Mercury

Monday

1. Venus	7. Sun
2. Mercury	8. Venus
3. Moon	9. Mercury
4. Saturn	10. Moon
5. Jupiter	11. Saturn
6. Mars	12. Jupiter

Tuesday

1. Saturn	7. Moon
2. Jupiter	8. Saturn
3. Mars	9. Jupiter
4. Sun	10. Mars
5. Venus	11. Sun
6. Mercury	12. Venus

Wednesday

1. Sun	7. Mars
2. Venus	8. Sun
3. Mercury	9. Venus
4. Moon	10. Mercury
5. Saturn	11. Moon
6. Jupiter	12. Saturn

Thursday

1. Moon	7. Mercury
2. Saturn	8. Moon
3. Jupiter	9. Saturn
4. Mars	10. Jupiter
5. Sun	11. Mars
6. Venus	12. Sun

Friday

1. Mars	7. Jupiter
2. Sun	8. Mars
3. Venus	9. Sun
4. Mercury	10. Venus
5. Moon	11. Mercury
6. Saturn	12. Moon

Saturday

1. Mercury	4. Jupiter	7. Venus	10. Saturn
2. Moon	5. Mars	8. Mercury	11. Jupiter
3. Saturn	6. Sun	9. Moon	12. Mars

Chapter 4

Divination Before Incantation

D ivination is an art that has been practiced in one form or another since ancient times and by all cultures. Both royalty and peasantry alike have looked to the mystical cards of the Tarot as well as to crystal gazing balls, scrying mirrors, runestones, dream-visions, and other methods to reveal the unknown and that which is yet to be.

Although divination extends well beyond the domain of Gypsies, prophets, and Witches, many spellcrafters faithfully embrace the divinatory arts as a means to determine the outcome of their spells. In fact, some modern Witches would never even think of invoking, incanting, or enchanting without first doing a preliminary divination.

Numerous methods of divination are employed and, naturally, every spellcaster has his or her own personal favorite. However, the oracle of choice among many magickal individuals remains the ever-popular Tarot.

The following are the 22 keys (cards) of the Major Arcana (trump cards) of the Tarot, along with interpretations for both their upright and reversed (that is, upside down) positions in relation to the casting of spells. They are presented for the benefit of the spellcrafter who desires to know beforehand if his or her spellwork will result in success or failure, and, perhaps more importantly, if it will backfire.

The divinatory meanings in this chapter are based on the traditional interpretations of the Tarot and are intended to offer insight and serve as a guide. However, in the art of divination, nothing is carved in stone. If you perform a reading and the cards strongly "speak" to you in an altogether different manner, it would probably be in your own best interest to follow what you feel in your heart to be true (your "gut feeling") and what you perceive through your "third eye." Using your own powers of intuition is the key to being successful in a Tarot reading, or in any other method of divination for that matter.

A man consults a Tarot reader. 14th-century illustration.
(Mary Evans Picture Library)

The 22 Keys of the Major Arcana

0—The Fool
1—The Magician
2—The High Priestess
3—The Empress
4—The Emperor
5—The Hierophant
6—The Lovers
7—The Chariot
8—Strength
9—The Hermit
10—Wheel of Fortune

11—Justice
12—The Hanged Man
13—Death
14—Temperance
15—The Devil
16—The Tower
17—The Star
18—The Moon
19—The Sun
20—Judgment
21—The World

Tarot Incantation and Divination

Before casting a spell, especially if it is one that you have mixed feelings about or if you are concerned that the outcome of your magick might produce negative repercussions, perform the following Tarot incantation and divination: Separate the 22 trump cards of the Major Arcana from the rest of the deck, setting the Minor Arcana aside. Holding the trump cards between the palms of your hands, repeat the following incantation to invoke the spirit of the Tarot to assist you in your reading:

> *Tarot, unto me reveal*
> *The outcome of my spell,*
> *Positive or negative,*
> *I thank thee for a sign to tell.*
> *I will shuffle and cut thrice,*
> *Then draw for the truth I seek.*
> *Through these mystic cards' advice*
> *0 spirit of the Tarot, speak.*

Shuffle the cards while focusing all of your thoughts upon your spell. Do not think about anything else.

Some Tarot diviners, especially those involved in the magickal arts, find that if they face East or West while reading the cards the divinatory energies raised are more conducive to an accurate reading. In magick, East is the direction traditionally associated with divination, and West is traditionally associated with clairvoyance and intuition.

When you feel that the cards are ready to give you the answer you seek, stop shuffling, cut them three times, and then either turn up the top card from the pile or spread out the cards on a table top and pick one card at random. This can be done with your eyes open or closed, depending upon which way feels right for you. Read the chosen card using the following Tarot interpretations for spellcrafters, and then give thanks in your own words to the spirit of the Tarot.

If the spellwork at hand is being considered by an entire coven rather than by a solitary Witch, it would be appropriate for the coven's High Priestess (or High Priest) to perform the divination with all coveners present and perhaps seated in a circle.

0—The Fool

Traditionally portraying a young man (sometimes clothed in the costume of a court jester) with his back turned towards the sun and about to blindly step off the edge of a high cliff, the unnumbered card of the Fool begins the Major Arcana of the Tarot.

The message of the Fool may be that you (the querant) need to take a more serious approach to your magick, that the spellwork you are contemplating will involve a risk of some sort, or that you need to be absolutely sure before working your magick that you have made the right decision in the matter.

The Fool often appears in the readings of novice Witches and magicians dabbling in magickal workings where there is a strong element of danger (such as Goetic evocations, necromancy, chaos magick, and the opening of Gates in Necronomicon rituals, just to give a few examples). Tampering with dark occult forces that you neither fully understand nor know how to control is foolish, and, in some cases, it can be deadly! Keep in mind that a little bit of knowledge can be a dangerous thing. Always act with wisdom and maturity in your Craft, harm none, and do as thou wilt.

When the Fool turns up in its reversed position, it generally indicates that unwise decisions have been, or will be, made. You would do well to think twice before proceeding with your spellwork.

I—The Magician

Indicating willpower, energy, the manipulative skills of a conjurer, all things of a magickal nature, and the ability to charm others, the Magician is one of the most auspicious cards in any spellcrafter's Tarot deck. When it turns up as a reply to a question regarding the outcome of a spell, it means that your goal—whatever it may be—will be achieved. It also reveals that, as a practitioner of the magickal arts, you are confident, skillful, and able to raise and direct great power. Sybil Leek once described the card of the Magician as "one of the most fortunate cards, which can be clearly associated with success."

In a reversed position, the Magician is said to indicate a lack of confidence or skill on the part of the person planning to cast the spell on which the Tarot reading is focused. Unless confidence is increased and/or magickal skills are fine-tuned, the chances of the spellworking to the sender's satisfaction are slim to none. In some instances, the reversed Magician points to a misuse of magickal energies or the manipulation of others through the art of enchantment or through occult trickery. Although it is true that all magick is manipulative to varying degrees, the deliberate interfering with another's free will—especially in any type of negative manner—usually comes at a karmic price.

2—The High Priestess

Hidden influences are often at work when the High Priestess appears in a reading. This card is also said to be extremely favorable for individuals involved in the arts or any form of mysticism. In addition, it symbolizes intuition, psychic powers and occult wisdom, and the power of the subconscious mind to affect self-transformation and self-healing. The High Priestess in her upright position denotes success in your magickal working, especially if it is connected with the arts, healing, clairvoyance, or personal transformations. If the spellcrafter is a man and his magick is to draw love, the High Priestess indicates that he will win the heart, or at the very least capture the attention, of the woman of his dreams.

When the card of the High Priestess appears in a reversed position, this should be taken as a warning not to proceed with your spellwork until your knowledge of magick and/or of the situation at hand has been expanded.

3—The Empress

The Empress is said to be the card of the Earth Mother, and in a reading it traditionally indicates such things as marriage, children, material wealth, and abundance in all human affairs.

If your spellwork involves fertility, the increase of money, marriage (or other unions), children, the home, farming or gardening, or the creative arts, the Empress is perhaps the best card to turn up in a reading.

However, when the Empress appears in a reversed position, this generally indicates failure, frustration, and unproductiveness. Check to see if your magick is properly timed and if you have all of the herbs, oils, and magickal paraphernalia necessary for the spellwork. If so, and if the Empress still appears reversed, take it as a warning that some obstacle (perhaps inexperience or lack of faith in one's magickal abilities, karmic energies, the universal plan, or the will of the gods) will prevent you from succeeding at this point in time.

The exception to this would be spells designed to cause abortion or infertility, domestic strife, separation, or divorce, in which case the Empress reversed would indicate successful results for the spellcaster.

4—The Emperor

The card of the Emperor signifies great power, strength, success, the fruits of labor, and the results of action. This is a favorable card for any spellcrafter, especially if the spellwork involves commanding, control over a situation, domination over others, physical strength, fatherhood, or avenging a wrongdoing.

In the reversed position, the Emperor may indicate a lack of power, direction, self-discipline, strength, or maturity on the part of the spellcrafter—all factors that can have an adverse effect on one's magickal efforts. It may also serve as an indication that the psychic or magickal powers of another are at work against you.

5—The Hierophant

Also known as the High Priest or the Pope, the Hierophant is a spiritual and powerful card. When it appears in a spellcrafter's reading, it may be trying to tell the querant that he or she should take the "tried and tested" magickal approach, follow the traditional laws of magick, adhere to the Wiccan Rede ("An' it harm none, do what thou wilt"), and look beyond the trappings of pomp and ceremony to gain a deeper understanding of the Inner Mysteries.

If you are experiencing difficulties or uncertainty regarding your spellwork, the Hierophant suggests seeking the advice of a magickal adept whose opinion and views you truly respect.

When the Hierophant appears in a reversed position, it indicates that an unconventional or unorthodox approach should be taken. Be receptive to new ideas, write and perform your own spells or rituals, and do not allow a fear of the disapproval of others to interfere with your magick.

6—The Lovers

The Lovers is perhaps the most auspicious card to appear in a Tarot reading pertaining to the outcome of a love spell. It signifies romance, courtship, commitment, and marriage, among other things. In its reversed position (pertaining to love magick) it indicates unrequited love, a lovers' quarrel, a separation, a divorce, or the ending of a love affair. Unless the goal of your amatory spell is to end a relationship or affair, counter another Witch's love enchantment, or free yourself from the painful feelings and confusing thoughts that chain you like a prisoner to a past or present relationship, the Lovers reversed means that your love spell will probably result in failure or rebound against you in a negative manner.

Aside from love magick, the Lovers card may indicate that the outcome of your spell will lead to a commitment, the overcoming of troubles, an emotional decision (not necessarily relating to romantic issues), or, on a deeper level, a conflict between the mind and the heart, virtue and vice, earthly pursuits and spiritual desires, and so forth.

In its reversed position, the card of the Lovers is a warning that you should postpone the casting of your spell until you have reevaluated the situation and given careful thought how to best deal with it. Take care not to make any hasty or ill-considered decisions.

7—The Chariot

The Chariot card is a good sign, indicating triumph, victory, and achievement. Your spell will put things into motion and success will be its final outcome. If your spell is one intended to break a curse, a jinx, or a streak of bad luck, the Chariot asserts that your troubles will be overcome.

If the Chariot appears in a Tarot reading in a reversed position, this means that if your spell is cast at this time, it will most likely result in failure or a false triumph. There is also the possibility that it may yield chaos or catastrophe for you. The reversed Chariot often appears when one has lost his or her sense of direction and purpose (two key factors to successful spellcrafting). Perhaps try a calmer, more organized approach. Make sure that you are incorporating the appropriate correspondences into your spell, and timing it for the proper lunar phase.

8—Strength

Also known as Fortitude or Force, the card of Strength is a favorable card in any reading, especially one pertaining to the outcome of any given spell the divinatory message conveyed by the maiden and her lion is that there is great power contained within the spell you are about to unleash. You are working with some very strong magick here. Strength also promises that spiritual power will triumph over material power.

If you are working to overcome obstacles, banish negativity in any form, dispel evil, increase strength (either on a physical or spiritual level), subdue passions, inspire courage or self-confidence, take charge of a situation, or gain power over another person, your spell is guaranteed to hit the target.

In its reversed position, the card of strength may be trying to tell you that the spell you plan to use is lacking the necessary strength to be effective or that your spellcasting skills need to be strengthened before attempting to work the magick. Strength reversed also points to the possibility of an abuse of magickal power, an attempt to employ force in order to gain one's ends, or negative thoughts that may interfere with the magickal process or permit obstacles (either actual or imaginary) to inhibit the spell's potency.

9—The Hermit

The Hermit, in the words of English Witch Sybil Leek, "is one of the most difficult cards in the pack." It must be interpreted very carefully and all things relating to the spell must be taken into careful consideration. The Hermit may indicate that the magickal operation would, for whatever reason, be better cast by a solitary practitioner rather than by an entire coven, or it may mean that meditation and more contemplation on the issue would be prudent before the spell is cast.

If your spell relates in some way to wisdom, knowledge, spirit guides, solitude, breaking bad habits, or a request for help, the presence of the Hermit in a reading is indeed a very good omen. It is not a favorable card, however, where readings pertaining to the outcome of love enchantments or spells to promote fertility are concerned.

In a reversed position, the Hermit means that your spell will likely result in feelings of alienation, loneliness, emotional or spiritual deprivation, a communication breakdown, isolation, or abandonment of some sort. It may also be trying to tell you that you are acting before thinking, regardless if you are motivated by the best of intentions.

10—The Wheel of Fortune

The Wheel of Fortune is one of the most powerful cards of both the Major and Minor Arcana of the Tarot, indicating good luck, new cycles, and major changes in the offing. When the Wheel of Fortune appears in a spellcrafter's reading, this is a strong indication that the spell will be met with success. This card is especially significant if the spellwork involves the changing of one's luck from bad to good, gambling and lotteries, gaining control over one's life, and achieving goals.

If the Wheel of Fortune appears in your reading in its reversed position, you would be wise to postpone your magickal working until a more auspicious time. There is a strong chance that, should you decide to carry out your spell despite the card's warning, you will meet failure or possibly even make the situation worse. Be prepared for setbacks and bad luck where magickal endeavors are concerned.

11—Justice

The card of Justice is said to be "one of the three virtues in the Major Arcana." (The cards of Strength and Temperance are the other two.) It is a very favorable card, indicating that justice will be served, lawsuits won, and balanced restored where there had previously been imbalance. If your spellwork focuses on legal matters, balance, decision making, business partnerships, or avenging a wrongdoing, the appearance of the Justice card in a Tarot reading is a good sign.

However, if the card of Justice turns up in its reversed position, it could indicate legal complications or the losing of a lawsuit. It may also be a warning against unfair judgments, excessive severity, victimization, and abuse of magickal power on the part of the spellcrafter. Use mercy and understanding when judging others. Justice reversed can also mean that a different approach (either on a magickal or mundane level) may be needed.

12—The Hanged Man

The card of the Hanged Man traditionally portrays a young man suspended by one foot from a T-cross made of living wood. His arms are folded behind his back and his head is surrounded by a brilliant halo.

When the Hanged Man appears in a spellcrafter's Tarot reading, it generally means that whatever spellwork was being contemplated should be postponed until a later time. There is good cause to wait and to be patient. This card may also be trying to tell you that a spell alone is not enough for you to achieve your desired goal. You will need to make some worthwhile sacrifices. This, of course, does not mean performing an animal or human bloodletting. Rather, it means that you must be willing to give something up or "surrender yourself to a Higher Authority" in order to get what you need or desire. As the Hanged Man is also connected to prophetic power, spiritual healing, and working with dreams, you may want to explore these paths or incorporate them into your future spellwork.

When the Hanged Man turns up in a reversed position, it indicates a resistance to spiritual influences, wasted effort, and false prophecy—none of which are very conducive to successful spellcrafting.

13—Death

The number 13 is traditionally regarded as unlucky, especially to Christians, because of the number's connection to the Last Supper. However, despite its gruesome symbols (that of a skeleton riding a white horse) and the fact that Death is the 13th key of the Tarot's Major Arcana, this card is normally not an indication of bad luck. In most cases it points to change, transformations, and endings followed by new beginnings. In very few cases does it warn against a death in the physical sense. However, if a curse on an enemy's health or a spell directed towards a gravely ill person was involved, this card could very well hold such a meaning. If you are considering casting a spell that involves a change in the course of one's life, replacement of something, or the bringing of something to a close, the card of Death is a good omen, indicating that your spell will yield successful results.

If Death is in a reversed position, it means that this is not an auspicious time for a change; you should refrain from casting any spells because all spells, bring about a change in one form or another. Death reversed may also mean that nothing will come of your spell should you proceed to perform it.

14—Temperance

The card of Temperance traditionally portrays an angelic being pouring liquid from one chalice into another, and speaks of finding the correct balance or mixture. For spellcrafters, this may be taken as a reference to a magick potion and finding the right ingredients to make it work.

Moderation and patience are two of the key words connected to Temperance, so keep this well in mind before working your magick, and avoid extremes. If your intent is to find harmony or restore balance, your spell will not fail you with Temperance on your side. In *The Sybil Leek Book of Fortune Telling*, the card of Temperance is said to mean that an individual "will have a good sense of timing, which will make actions successful." Keeping this in mind, see to it that your spell is set for the right day and hour, as the proper timing (working in harmony with lunar phases and planetary hours) is one of the keys to successful magick.

In the reversed position, Temperance indicates imbalance, negative emotions, impatience, unfortunate combinations, lack of self control, inconsistency of purpose, and frequent changes of mind—all of which are negative things that can contaminate your magickal energies and diminish the effectiveness of your intended spell.

"Things connected with churches, religion, [and] sects" is another meaning attributed to Temperance reversed, according to Arthur Edward Waite's *The Pictorial Key of the Tarot*. For a spellcrafter, such things could very well be candles, incense, altar tools, amulets and talismans, consecrations, Pagan deities, and so forth. Make sure that you have all the required ingredients for magick before attempting to put your spell into motion.

15—The Devil

If the intent of your spell is to bind a person from doing harm to others (as well as to himself), to conjure forth intense feelings of lust or rage in another, or to enslave someone (to an idea or a relationship, for example), the Devil indicates that you will succeed in your magickal workings. This ominous-looking card often appears when malevolent magick is being employed. It may also serve as a warning against the threat of possession, temptation, or evil influences connected with your spellwork.

If your intent is to escape from unpleasant or frustrating circumstances, break a jinx, counter a curse or hex, or free yourself from someone or something (such as a bad habit or addiction), the devil card means there is a good chance that your spell will not bring you the results you seek.

When the card of the Devil appears in its reversed position in a reading, it is generally believed to be a good sign. It signifies liberation, a release from burdens of the past, the power to overthrow evil or keep unlucky influences at bay, success in removing curses and jinxes, and a chance to eliminate undesirable elements or individuals. Finally, the Devil reversed means failure for the casting of any spell that falls under the category of black magick.

16—The Tower

The lightning-struck Tower is not a very favorable card for indicating the outcome of any well-intended spell. Also known as the Falling Tower or the House of God, it signifies disaster, calamity, misfortune, misery, disruption, accidents, distress, disgrace, ruin, sudden and drastic changes, and events of a shocking and disturbing nature. Unless your spell is designed to bring about any of the aforementioned, you would be well-advised to call off your spellwork. Arthur Edward Waite described the Tower as "a card in particular of unforeseen catastrophe."

In a reversed position, the card of the Tower retains the same meanings as above, but to a lesser degree of severity. However, caution where spellcrafting is concerned should not be thrown to the wind, for even in this position the Tower is regarded as a card possessing great karmic significance. Bear in mind that in the art of magick, energy sent equals energy returned. (And among many who follow the path of Wicca, this energy, whether positive or negative, is believed to rebound upon the sender threefold or greater.)

17—The Star

The Star is a favorable card for spellcrafters, for when it appears in a Tarot reading it indicates a strong possibility that the goal of your spell—regardless of what it may be—will be manifest. Also known as the "wish card," the Star is a sign that you will get your wish, so be careful what you wish for! Traditionally, the Star also indicates healing and a return to health (either physically or spiritually), so if your spell pertains in any way to healing and health, this card predicts an especially positive outcome.

The positive quickly turns to the negative when the Star appears in a reversed position, for all of the promising aspects of the upright card now hold the opposite meaning. It is doubtful that your wish will be granted or your goal achieved at this time or through the particular spell you have chosen to utilize. Be prepared for disappointment if you decide to proceed with your magick despite the card's warning.

The most positive message that can be spelled out by the Star reversed is the slight possibility that the spell will work, but only partially or perhaps after a long delay or setback. There is also a good possibility that the predicted failure of the spell will be the direct or indirect result of the spellcrafter's own self-created obstacles, such as feelings of pessimism, lack of conviction or motivation, self-doubt, a fear of failure or of the unknown, a negative attitude, and so forth. Once realized, such obstacles can be overcome if one sets his or her mind and heart to it.

18—The Moon

The card of the Moon, which traditionally portrays a face in the moon gazing down between two twin towers upon a pair of howling hounds while a crayfish emerges from the waters, is a card of strong Hecate energy. It is connected to dreams, visions, intuition and psychic powers, occult forces, illusions, and deceptions. If any of these attributes is connected with your spellwork and the Moon turns up in your Tarot reading, this may be taken as a favorable sign. The Moon also represents that which is mysterious and hidden; therefore, it may be a reminder to be secretive about one's spellwork if it is to achieve success.

It is interesting to point out that the Moon is the 18th key of the Major Arcana, and in numerology 18 translates to nine, which has been called "the number of perfection." The number nine, being the result of the number three (a number linked to the Triple Goddess, the Holy Trinity, moon-magick, pyramid power, and the triangle) multiplied by itself, is said to be the most sacred and magickal of all numbers. Numerologists also add occult significance to the number nine because no matter which other digit the number nine is multiplied by, the digits of the resulting number will always add up to nine.

In a reversed position, the card of the Moon may indicate that the phase of the moon or the astrological sign that it is currently in is not the most favorable for the type of magick you intend to perform. It can also denote hidden fears that may prevent the spellcrafter from reaching his or her full magickal potential. Such fears need to be confronted and controlled before proceeding with one's spellwork.

19—The Sun

The card of the Sun is one of the most auspicious cards in the Major Arcana, indicating that success, achievement, or attainment is forthcoming. The other meanings attributed to the Sun include happiness, positive energy, enlightenment, good luck, the overcoming of obstacles, material wealth, happy marriages, and contentment. In a reading where a yes or no question has been asked, the Sun is always an affirmative answer.

When this card turns up in its reversed position, it indicates that, for one reason or another, the spell that you are planning to cast will end in failure. The Sun reversed is especially unlucky when love enchantment is involved, for it generally is an indication of marital woes, broken engagements, separations, or divorces in the offing.

20—Judgment

The card of Judgment, also known as the Angel, traditionally portrays the angel Gabriel blowing on his trumpet as the naked dead rise from their coffins below. This is a very karmic card, and its message is "as ye sow, so shall ye reap." For Wiccans and many other contemporary Pagans, this may translate into a reminder not to lose sight of the Wiccan Rede when spellcasting and to be ever mindful of the Threefold Law, which states that three times the positive or the negative energy you send out is returned to you. (Or, in other words, what goes around comes around—thrice!)

In its reversed position, the card of Judgment often indicates an outcome with unsatisfactory results. It may also hold the message that there is nothing now that can be done on a magickal level to improve the situation at hand. It may be best for you to accept what cannot (or should not) be changed, and then look to the future and move on.

21—The World

The card of the World traditionally portrays a skyclad dancing maiden holding a wand in each hand. She is surrounded by a magick circle in the form of a wreath of leaves, and at the four corners are four "beasts," which represent the four Elements of Air, Fire, Water, and Earth in perfect balance. The World is the most fortuitous of all the cards of both the Major and the Minor Arcana. It symbolizes completion, a job well done, cosmic knowledge, achievement, the end of one's journey, success, material and spiritual manifestations, mastering the world as opposed to being mastered by it, and the perpetual cycle of life, death, and rebirth in both a physical and spiritual sense.

For a spellcrafter, the appearance of the world in a Tarot reading indicates that he or she will be triumphant in the magickal endeavor. Whatever the goal of the spell, it shall be achieved.

In its reversed position, the card of the World warns that a strong probability of failure, recurring problems, delays, and obstacles exists at this time. Postpone your spellwork until a more favorable time. In some cases, the World reversed indicates that steps have already been taken to resolve the problem or to bring the matter to closure.

Chapter 5

Amulets, Talismans, Charms, and Fetishes

Although amulets, talismans, charms, and fetishes, appear to be similar in many ways and are often confused, there is a significant difference between each one and the ways in which it works.

Since primitive times, man has invested faith in the power of various magickal objects, which we now call amulets, charms, and so forth. The use of these objects appears to be universal, and within the framework of the magickal arts, the use of fetishes and charms is connected mainly to the practice of Low Magick; talismans to the practice of High Magick; and amulets to both.

In *The Complete Book of Amulets and Talismans*, author Migene Gonzalez-Wippler states that amulets and talismans can change the circumstances surrounding our lives, but only if we put our faith in them. It is this faith that is the "true power behind amulets and talismans."

Man-made Amulets

According to first century Roman author Pliny, an amulet is "an object that protects a person from trouble." Amulets can be either nature-made or man-made objects, and the most common types are horseshoes, a rabbit's foot, jewelry, stones (especially those that traditionally correspond to a person's astrological sign or month of birth), bones, seashells, and horns (popular among people of Italian heritage).

In Mesopotamia, animal-shaped amulets were popular among the Sumerians and Babylonians, and were commonly used for fertility, strength, and protection. The oldest of these amulets dates back to about 2500 B.C. Cylinder seals fashioned from precious or semiprecious stones engraved with prayers and religious scenes were also used for various purposes. Other amulets used by the Sumerians and Babylonians, and in later times by the Assyrians, included figures of male and female deities, reptiles, and curious winged beings with human-like bodies and leonine heads.

In ancient Egypt, where majestic pyramids filled with secrets dominated the warm desert sands, numerous animal-headed gods and goddesses were worshipped. The sacred names of these deities, along with their divine images, were commonly inscribed upon amulets. Those that had received a magician's blessing were believed to be especially potent.

The oldest of Egyptian amulets is the ankh, which symbolized life and was sacred to all deities of the pantheon. Also known as the Key to the Nile and, to the early Christians, as an "ansated cross," the ankh was believed to ensure the immortality of every god and goddess, who were nearly always depicted in works of art carrying the symbol in their right hands.

Ankh amulets of ancient Egypt were fashioned from such materials as wood, stone, various metals, and even wax. Consisting of a male symbol (the cross) surmounted by a female symbol (an oval), it clearly represented the sacred union of God and Goddess, whose marriage was said to take place at the source of the River Nile each year prior to the flood.

Other important amulets of the ancient Egyptians included the scarab (in the shape of a dung-eating beetle, which symbolized resurrection of the dead and eternal life, and was worn for protection against all forms of evil); the udjat (also known as the Eye of Horus, which was also worn for protection, repelling the evil eye, promoting good health, and general well-being); and the serpent's head (which protected the living from cobras and other poisonous snakes, and protected the dead from the serpent of the Underworld). The nefer, an amulet bearing a slight resemblance to a miniature lute, was greatly valued for its power to bestow upon its wearer physical strength, youth, good luck, and joy. Amulets in the shape of a frog were sacred to the goddess Hequit, and were used to ensure female fertility. Vulture-shaped amulets were carried by those in need of strength and fierceness. The tjet was an amulet associated with the goddess Isis, and was normally fashioned from red glass, red wood, or a red-colored gemstone such as jasper or carnelian. It was believed to bestow upon its wearer the powers of the sacred blood of Isis.

The Seal of Solomon (also known as the six-pointed Star of David) is a powerful magickal symbol that appeared on many ancient Hebrew amulets. In the Middle Ages, it was believed to offer its owner protection from enemies, lethal weapons, and fire. Although it is the most prominent symbol of Judaism, the six-pointed star predates the Jewish religion and was, at one time, used as a magickal symbol by magicians in Egypt, Babylonia, and Assyria.

The Hebrews were known to have employed a wide variety of amulets, which are mentioned throughout the Bible. Many of these amulets, such as phylacteries (leather frontlets containing strips of parchment inscribed with the Shema Ysrael prayer), bells (to ward off evil spirits), and tzitzit (a sacred tassle or fringe), were worn on the garments of the High Priests. The letters of the Hebrew alphabet were also regarded as powerful amulets by the ancient Hebrews, for each was thought to contain magickal powers.

The mezuzah is a small cylinder that contains a tiny strip of parchment upon which is inscribed certain Biblical passages. It is traditionally affixed to a door frame to protect the house and the family who dwells within it from demons and evil ghosts. Although generally associated with Judaism, the use of door charms actually originated in ancient Egypt, where sacred tablets engraved with hieroglyphic spells and known as Pillars of Horus were attached to doors to prevent the spirits of the dead from gaining entrance to a house and haunting or possessing the living.

However, the greatest Hebrew amulet was the Torah (or Book of the Law). Miniature versions were commonly worn on a chain around the neck and used to keep all manners of evil at bay and protect the wearer from harm. It was also used to safeguard pregnant women during childbirth and was placed in or near cribs to heal children suffering from an illness. The custom of wearing a miniature Torah for amuletic purposes is one that continues to be observed by many Orthodox Jews throughout the world.

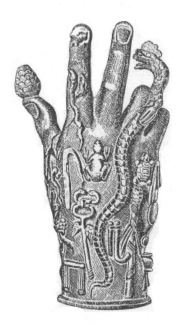

A powerful hand-shaped amulet used by the ancient Egyptians to avert the evil eye. (The British Museum, London)

An interesting amulet once used in Arabia for protection against evil consisted of a small pouch filled with dust gathered from tombs. The pouch would be blessed by special prayers, empowered by having magickal names ritually recited over it, and then worn.

A phallus-shaped amulet known as a baskanion, a probaskanion, or a fascinum was widely used in ancient Greece as a magickal device to ward off the evil eye. This protective amulet was not only worn on necklaces, but mounted on houses and black-smith forges, displayed in gardens, and even affixed to the wheels of chariots. A similar amulet was used in Rome, where it was called a Satyrica sigma.

Natural Amulets

Natural amulets are created by Mother Nature and are said to possess power and good luck. Natural amulets include: trees, plants, flowers, herbs, vegetables, fruits, stones (ordinary, precious, and semiprecious), metals, lodestones, soil, sand, rock, organic substances (such as amber, ambergris, coral, ivory, pearl, and so on), animals, fish, birds, insects, and even human beings.

Examples of human amulets that have been used probably since the Stone Age are: locks of hair, teeth, fingernail clippings, umbilical cords, cauls (a membrane that covers the head of some infants at birth), skulls, shrunken heads, and even bodily fluids (particularly blood, menstrual blood, saliva, and semen).

Symbolic human amulets popularly include hands, eyes, hearts, and male genitals—all of which are reputed to contain potent magickal powers that act to counter to the effects of the evil eye.

Gypsy Amulets

The Gypsies believe very strongly in the malevolent powers of the evil eye, or the Berufen ("eye enchantment") as they call it. It is hardly surprising, therefore, that the majority of Gypsy amulets are designed to offer protection against it.

Bells, fans, whistles, tassles, coins, seashells, garlic, and snake symbols have all been used to prevent the evil eye from inflicting its harm. Mirrors are believed by many Gypsies to be highly effective amulets against the Berufen, because they reflect the gaze of the evil eye back to its sender.

The Pentacle

The most powerful of all amulets used by contemporary Pagans, Witches, and Wiccans is the silver pentacle. When its image is placed upon a ring or pendant, the five-pointed star protects the wearer against negative and evil influences. The pentacle is also used to symbolize positive power and to control the elemental forces of nature.

As an amulet of ceremonial magick, the pentacle is used for protection against attack from demons and spirits. Ceremonial magicians also use the five-pointed star as a talisman to evoke and control demons and spirits.

The five-pointed star is the most powerful of all Pagan and magickal symbols.

Fetishes

In African primitive magick, the most powerful of all amulets is the fetish, which is also called a ju-ju or a gris-gris, among many other names. Formed naturally by Mother Nature or artificially by the hands of a shaman or Witch doctor, fetishes are believed to be possessed by spirits, which give the objects their magickal powers. Fetishes are used mainly for protection against evil, disease, bad luck, sorcery, accidents, and death.

Webster's New Encyclopedia of Dictionaries describes a fetish as "an object or image superstitiously invested with divine or demoniac power, and, as such, reverenced devoutly." The word "fetish" derives from the Portuguese feitico, which translates to "magick."

The most common form of fetish found in West Africa is the wooden doll. Fetishes also take the form of animals, teeth, the bones of snakes, and beautifully decorated stones, all of which are worn on the body or carried in charm bags.

Charms

In the art of spellcrafting, there exist three very distinct types of charms: amuletic, verbal, and written. The first is akin to the amulet and can be any natural or man-made object that is used mainly to attract good luck or to "charm" or subjugate others. Most charms of this type are worn as jewelry or carried in small drawstring pouches called charm bags.

In medieval times, the Catholic Church promoted the use of numerous holy charms, despite the fact that it vehemently disapproved of all Pagan magick. Christian charms included rosaries, holy relics, the Scriptures, and a small wax cake known as an Agnus Dei, which was decorated with images of the lamb (the totemic symbol of Jesus Christ) and the flag. Holy charms were blessed by priests or the Pope, and worn to protect against such things as evil ghosts, demons, the Devil, fire, thunder, lightning, tempests, fever, drowning, and death during childbirth.

The second type of charm consists of magickal words, phrases, chants, and incantations. Verbal (or spoken) charms have been uttered since ancient times and continue to be employed by many practitioners of folk magick in the 21st century. Verbal charms are traditionally recited during spells and other magick-related activities, including the consecration of altars and ritual tools, the harvesting of magickal herbs, the brewing of potions, and so forth. For nearly every desire and need, there exists a charm.

An example of a 19th-century English charm to protect against sorcery is as follows:

> *He who forges images,*
> *He who bewitches*
> *The malevolent aspect,*
> *The evil eye,*
> *The malevolent lip,*
> *The finest sorcery,*
> *Spirit of the Heavens,*
> *Conjure it!*
> *Spirit of the Earth,*
> *Conjure it!*

In medieval times it was common for charmers to recite Christian prayers in Latin to cure and to protect against evil in its many guises. But perhaps the most infamous of all spoken charms connected to Christianity was the backwards recitation of the Paternoster (or Lord's Prayer), which was believed to summon forth the Devil from his infernal realm of fire and darkness.

During the Burning Times in Europe, Witches were routinely accused of reciting the Pasternoster in reverse at Sabbats or while driving a coffin nail into the footprint of an enemy to bring harm or death to him or her. Churchmen of that era claimed that the reason Witches spoke the prayer backwards was because the Devil (to whom the prayer was greatly offensive) did not permit his followers to recite it from start to finish. Thus, if an accused Witch on trial could not recite the entire Paternoster perfectly and without difficulty or the forgetting of a single word, she would be found, beyond the shadow of a doubt, guilty by the jury and condemned to hang from the gallows until dead or roasted alive at the stake.

The third type of charm utilizes the magickal power of words and names (especially those of spirits, demons, and deities), which are traditionally written upon parchment and worn on the body. Typically, a written charm will contain a prayer, phrase, or magickal formula, and will often require being spoken a certain number of times and/or during a particular planetary hour in order to be effective.

One of the oldest, and perhaps the most well-known, of all written charms in recorded history is the Abracadabra, which at one time was widely believed to possess curative powers. When written on parchment, worn around the patient's neck on a chain or string, and then recited out loud in the same diminishing manner as written, the charm is supposed to banish a fever.

The origin of the word "abracadabra" is very mysterious; the theory that suggests it derived from the ancient Chaldean phrase "abbada ke dabra," which roughly translates to "perish like the word," seems to be the most probable. Its use as a magickal charm can be traced as far back as the second century, and some occult historians surmise that it was invented by the physician Serenus Sammonicus to cure the fever of the Roman emperor Caracalla.

Talismans

Talismans are often confused with amulets, and vice versa. *Webster's New Encyclopedia of Dictionaries* defines a talisman as "an object endowed with magical power of protecting the wearer from harm; a lucky charm." It also defines an amulet as "a talisman." No wonder there is so much confusion as to what constitutes a talisman and what constitutes an amulet.

According to Susan Bowes in *Notions and Potions*, "Talismans have been used as magical charms to attract wealth, harmony, and happiness, as opposed to amulets, which repel or protect."

Talismans are always prepared for a specific reason, and can enable powerful transformations, whereas amulets serve a general purpose—typically attracting good luck and warding off evil. Another difference between talismans and amulets is that talismans require a magickal "charging" by a Witch or magician in order to endow them with supernatural power. An amulet, on the other hand, is said to be naturally endowed with magickal properties. According to the laws of High Magick, a talisman can be empowered only by nature's forces, by deities, angels, or demons, or by being fashioned in a ritualistic manner.

Both talismans and amulets can be worn in the form of magickal jewelry, carried in charm bags with or without other magickal items, and used in working rituals in various ways.

The word "talisman" is said to derive either from the Greek word telesma (meaning "mystery" or "initiation") or the Greek root teleo (meaning "to consecrate"). From this derives the Arabic word tilsam (meaning "a magickal image").

Like amulets, talismans are connected to all cultures throughout recorded history. However, nowhere in the ancient world were they more popular than in Egypt and Babylonia, where the magickal arts played an important role in both religion and culture. The Egyptians employed talismans not only for magickal purposes, but also in funerary rites designed to safely guide the spirits of the dead across the threshold of death.

Magick seals, planetary pentacles, and magick squares (also known as kameas) are the most common types of talismans used by ceremonial magicians, and many of the ancient grimoires from centuries gone by contain detailed instructions on the making, consecration, and magickal application of such talismans. However, talismans can come in any size or shape, such as the magick wand of a wizard, the legendary sword of King Arthur (known as the Excalibur), the elusive Philosopher's Stone of the alchemists, and the helmet of invisibility worn by the Roman god Mercury. Even the severed hands of criminals were once used as talismans by practitioners of black magick in the Middle Ages.

One of the most famous of all talismans is the 16th-century medal of Catherine de Medici, a queen and consort of Henri II of France, who was known for being a devout believer in the occult arts. Made from metals that had been melted together under astrologically auspicious signs and blended with the blood of both man and goat, the medal bore on one side a Venus figure surrounded by the names of various demons. On the other side was an engraving of the supreme Roman god Jupiter, the eagle of

Ganymede (Cupbearer to the Gods), and a demonic jackal-headed figure thought to be the Egyptian underworld god and judge of the dead, Anubis. The medal, which was destroyed upon Catherine de Medici's death, was believed to have given the queen clairvoyance and sovereign power. A replica of the talisman is on display at the Bibliotheque Nationale in Paris.

According to occult legend, the magickal power of a talisman stays in effect for a period of time consisting of a year and one day—the same amount of time that many Witchcraft traditions require a novice Witch to study and train before being initiated into a coven. Some grimoires, however, claim that the "magickal lifespan" of a talisman is three, five, seven, or nine years. After a talisman has satisfied the needs or desires of the magician, or after its energy has dissipated, it is traditionally laid to rest in the soil of Mother Earth or cast into the ocean.

Talismanic Correspondences

Magickal correspondences play a vital role in the crafting of talismans. For a talisman to be truly effective, it must be made from a material (such as a metal or gemstone) that is ruled by the planet whose influence is desired. It must also be made during the day of the week, planetary hour, and phase of the moon corresponding to the magickal work at hand.

If a talisman is drawn on parchment, rather than etched upon metal or stone, the background of the parchment should be painted with the correct planetary color, and the magickal inscriptions should be done in black ink or paint. In the case of Saturn talismans, which are of the planetary color black, white is the appropriate complementary color to use for drawing symbols and writing names of power upon the black parchment.

The following is a list of the planets, their corresponding days, metals, colors, gemstones, and spheres of influence. (For planetary hours, see Chapter 3.) These correspondences have been applied to the crafting of talismans since ancient times.

The Sun

Day of the week: Sunday

Metal: Gold

Color: Yellow

Gemstones: Amber, hyacinth, topaz

Spheres of influence: Ambition, authority, career, fame, good fortune, healing, health, high office, honors, hope, legal matters, money, positions of rank and title, prosperity, protection, publicity, sports.

The Moon

Day of the week: Monday

Metal: Silver

Color: Violet or purple

Gemstones: Crystals, mother-of-pearl, opal

Spheres of influence: Administration, childbirth, children, clairvoyance, deliveries, feminine qualities, fertility, healing, home, intuition, maternity, peace, prophetic dreams, psychic powers, public contact, sleep, telepathy, travel by sea, visions.

Mars

Day of the week: Tuesday

Metal: Iron

Color: Red

Gemstones: Bloodstone, hematite, ruby

Spheres of influence: Chemistry, courage, destruction, exorcism, fire-fighting, health, hex-breaking, law enforcement, lust, masculine qualities, matrimony, medicine, military success, power over enemies, protection, self-defense, sexual energy, strength, surgery, valor, war, weapons.

Mercury

Day of the week: Wednesday

Metal: Mercury*

Color: Orange

Gemstones: Agate, carnelian, sardonyx

Spheres of influence: Acting, advice, bookkeeping, communication, divination, eloquence, healing (physical and psychic), literature, mental agility, mental health, messages, publishing, secretarial work, teaching, travel, wisdom, writing.

Caution: Mercury, also known as quicksilver, is extremely toxic! For this reason many spellcrafters prefer to work with a seal of mercury in the form of a parchment talisman rather than working with the actual metal associated with this planet.

Jupiter

Day of the week: Thursday

Metal: Tin

Color: Blue

Gemstones: Amethyst, sapphire, turquoise

Spheres of influence: Banking, business, desires, employers, finances, foreign affairs, honors, insurance, judgments, law, legal matters, luck, missionary work, money, political power, prosperity, religion, shipping, speculation, wealth.

Venus

Day of the week: Friday

Metal: Copper

Color: Green

Gemstones: Emerald, jade

Spheres of influence: Art, beauty, culture, the environment, femininity, fidelity, friendship, love, music, pleasure, romance, youth.

Saturn

Day of the week: Saturday

Metal: Lead

Color: Black

Gemstones: Jet, obsidian, onyx

Spheres of influence: Agriculture, animals and birds, death, endings, exorcism, farming, inheritance, karma, land, longevity, magickal herb gardens, mining, old age, property, protection, servants, visions, wills and legacies.

S	A	T	O	R
A	R	E	P	O
T	E	N	E	T
O	P	E	R	A
R	O	T	A	S

Several examples of ancient talismans. With the exception of the Sator word square (in the center), these talismans are from a late 18th-century grimoire known as the Black Pullet, *which is believed to have been written in Rome.*

Chapter 6

The Magick of Wax and Wick

Candle History and Lore

Throughout the world, candles have long played an important role in religious worship, folklore, divination, and the magickal arts. The soft, mellow glow of candlelight can help to put lovers in a romantic mood. It can also be used to conjure spirits (either of a benevolent or a malevolent nature), invoke gods and goddesses, and create magick.

Candle magick utilizes the ancient and highly powerful Element of Fire, which has been regarded as the sacred Element of magickal transformation since times most ancient.

The candle's origin is unknown; however, there exists evidence that the use of beeswax candles in Egypt and the island of Crete dates back as far as 3000 B.C. Other candles used in early times consisted of tallow-saturated rushes. In the 3rd century A.D., candles and lamps were utilized in Egypt as tools of divination.

In rituals known as "dreaming true," which were traditionally carried out in the darkness of caves, a diviner would face South and gaze into the flame until the vision of a divine being materialized before him. The diviner would then fall into a deep, sleep-like trance and receive the answers he sought in a prophetic dream.

By the 4th century, candles had found their way into the rites performed by followers of Christianity. However, they did not become a permanent fixture on church altars until the 12th century. The Catholic Church in the Middle Ages employed consecrated holy candles in exorcisms and rituals of blessings and absolving sins. They were also believed to be beneficial "for preserving oneself from the injury of witches" according to the infamous inquisitors' handbook known as the *Malleus Maleficaru* (1486).

Throughout Europe during what is now known as the Burning Times, it was commonly believed that witches lit candles at their Black Masses as offerings of fealty to the Prince of Darkness. The Devil was commonly depicted in works of art as a goat-headed creature sporting a lighted black candle between his horns. And it is said that it was from the flame of this most evil of candles that his followers lit their candles for black magick and necromancy.

Throughout the world, candles have long played an important role in religious worship, folklore, divination, and the magickal arts.
(Photo by Gerina Dunwich)

Witch-fearing Europeans of that era also believed that old hags and young enchantresses alike placed enchanted candles in the faggots of their besoms (brooms), which they used to aerially transport themselves to and from their Sabbat gatherings.

In the 16th century, an English work called *Dives and Pauper* revealed one way in which those who practiced black magick were able to lay a powerful curse upon their enemies with prayer and candle. According to one passage: "It hath oft been known that witches, with saying of the Paternoster and dropping of the holy candle on a man's steps that they hated, hath done his feet rotten of."

By the 17th century, those skilled in the Black Arts were said to have crafted special candles with the fat of unbaptised children and executed felons. It was believed that such candles contained life energy and therefore were regarded as extremely powerful tools of magick.

Many grimoires (magickal textbooks) from that period in history contained instructions for making candles out of human tallow and spells for their use. Usually they were employed for bringing the deceased back to life and discovering the location of hidden treasure, which was often guarded by the spirits of dead men.

An 18th-century grimoire known as the *Petit Albert* revealed to the world the secret of how a "magic candle" made of human tallow could be employed to find the spot where a treasure had been secretly buried. Consecrated and then enchanted by powerful occult incantations, a magic candle would be placed in the center of a horseshoe-shaped holder fashioned from the wood of the hazel (a tree long associated with diviners, Witches, and the supernatural). It would then be carried into a cave or subterranean location where treasure was suspected to be. When treasure was near, the candle's flame would sparkle brightly and emit loud hissing sounds similar to the sounds of an angry serpent. The closer one drew to the treasure, the brighter the magic candle burned and the louder it hissed.

By the same token, the dimming of the candle's flame would tell the treasure hunter that his search was leading him in the wrong direction. When the magic candle sensed the exact spot where the treasure lay hidden, its intense flame would suddenly extinguish on its own accord, as though being smothered out by some unseen snuffer.

In addition to the human tallow candles, diviners of treasure would carry with them candles of wax that had received blessings. These candles not only served to provide illumination after the flame of the magic candle went out, they offered protection against the spirits that were believed to guard all buried treasure.

An early 19th-century work called *The Magus,* written by Francis Barret, said that candles made of "some saturnine things, such as a man's fat and marrow, the fat of a black cat, with the brains of a crow or raven, which being extinguished in the mouth of a man lately dead, will afterwards, as often as it shines alone, bring great horror and fear upon the spectators about it."

After the repeal of England's Witchcraft Act in 1951 and the publication of Gerald Gardner's first two nonfiction books about the Craft (*Witchcraft Today* and *The Meaning of Witchcraft*), public interest in occultism and the Old Religion began to grow. The practice of Witchcraft soon experienced a revival as a Neo-Pagan religion, incorporating ancient Pagan rites, Goddess worship, and elements of European folklore and ceremonial magick.

The vast majority of the women and men who identify themselves as contemporary Witches seek to live in harmony with Mother Nature and use their magickal powers only for doing good. Crystals and herbs are commonly employed in magickal workings, and one of the most popular practices among both covens and solitaries the world over is the art of candle magick.

The dancing flame of a candle emits mystical power and is ideal for setting the proper atmosphere for casting spells, divining the future, meditating, and banishing darkness. As I wrote in my book, *The Magick of Candleburning,* "The symbolism of creating light in darkness also lies behind the use of the candle in rituals of magick." In addition, the candle serves as an image of humanity. Its wax is said to correspond to the physical body; its wick to the mind; and its flame to the spirit or soul.

Most modern Witches find candle magick to be uncomplicated and fun, yet incredibly powerful when performed with intent. It is a branch of magick that can help an individual to attract a compatible lover, land the right job, change bad luck into good, and even increase wealth. The flame of a magickally empowered candle can also be utilized for self-improvement, healing, banishing negativity, protection against evil forces, and so forth.

But, most importantly, candle magick can open the door to spiritual realms and other worlds, and serve to connect a human being with God/Goddess.

Candles and the Dead

Candles have long played an important role in the rites of the dead. In Ireland it is still customary for many families to surround the corpse of a deceased loved one with a dozen burning candles to protect it from marauding demons. According to Christian folklore, 12 candles are used because 12 is the number of the prophets and the apostles and therefore has the power to repel the hordes of hell. Additionally, the flames of the candles represent the sacred light of God.

Candles and the Devil

The popular expression "to hold a candle to the Devil" alludes to an old legend that hails from Ireland. On a day when Christians annually observed the Feast of Saint Michael, an old woman went to church to light two candles—one for the saint, and the other for the dragon he conquered. This aroused the curiosity of the priest, who asked the woman for an explanation. With a smile she replied that she wasn't sure if her soul would be bound for heaven or for hell after death, so she was seeing to it that she had a friend in both places!

Dreams

According to Nerys Dee's *The Dreamer's Workbook,* to dream about a lighted candle indicates strength and life. Candlelight also "reflects high ideals and throws a light on spiritual matters and understanding." However, a dream in which there is an unlit candle serves as a warning of deprivation and disappointment. Some dream interpreters believe that a candle in a dream is an omen of good luck and prosperity. Others regard it as a sacred symbol representing the inner light of the dreamer's soul. If the flame of the candle is snuffed out or blown out by the wind, such a dream is said to herald sorrowful news. A broken candle warns of bad luck and misfortune.

The colors of candles in dreams are said to hold great divinatory significance, as does the number of the candles. For instance, a white candle is an indication of the faithfulness of one's lover or spouse. A candle as red as the blood of life indicates intense desires or a return to radiant health. A green candle portends money or fertility. And death, illnesses, or evil influences are said to be foretold by candles as black as the darkness of the grave.

For a woman hoping to receive a proposal of marriage, a dream in which two (or five) white candles appear is a good sign that her amatory wishes will soon come true. However, if the candles she dreams about are black, this is a most ominous sign, indicating an unhappy marital union or quite possibly her widowhood.

The Pagan Roots of Birthday Candles

The popular custom of lighting candles on a birthday cake, making a wish, and then blowing out the candles is one that is carried out in many parts of the world. Most people are unaware, however, that this custom is actually the remnants of an age-old Pagan ritual. In ancient Greece, Artemis (virgin goddess of the hunt, lunar deity, and Greek equivalent to the Roman goddess Diana) was honored each year on the 24th day of May, the date of her birth, according to Greek mythology. In special temples consecrated to her worship, moon-shaped cakes adorned with burning candles would be placed upon the altar as offerings.

After the advent of the Christian faith in Greece, the worship of the ancient gods was banned by law and their temples destroyed or converted to the uses of the New Religion. However, many of the old ways, including the lighting of candles on birthday cakes, managed to survive into the present day.

Voodoo Candles

On the tropical island of Haiti, where the mysterious and centuries-old practice of Voodoo is widespread, candles have long played an important role in the casting of spells of both black and white magick and in the invocation of the loas, Voodoo deities who possess their devotees in frenzied ceremonies.

Voodoo rituals to conjure the spirits of the dead and to reanimate corpses as zombies call for the necromancer to go to the dead person's grave and light three candles at the foot of its cross. Glass-encased candles representing the Christian saints are popular spellcrafting tools among practitioners of Voodoo candle magick in the United States. Human image candles are equally popular and often used in the same fashion as the infamous Voodoo doll, being inscribed with the victim's name and pierced with pins while being burned upon an altar.

A Spellcaster's Guide to Candle Magick

As the 21st century dawns and the Age of Aquarius nears, the art and practice of candle magick remains one of the most popular forms of spellcraft among Witches and Wiccans alike. However, it is a craft that can be put to use by any magickally-inclined individual, regardless of his or her cultural background or spiritual beliefs. One does not necessarily need to be descended from a long line of Witches, belong to a coven, or be initiated into any Mystery Cults in order to work enchantments through the simple magick of wax and wick.

Candle magick falls under the category of Low Magick, which mainly concerns the lower or material planes, as opposed to the formal and often-complicated ceremonies of High Magick, which essentially involve invocations and evocations, and mainly concern the higher or mental planes. Candle magick, which combines the power of the two ancient and mighty Elements of Fire and Air, has been performed in Pagan shrines since pre-Christian times. Nearly every culture has known the magick of candles in one form or another. And even the Catholic Church has had its own versions of candle magick, including the old tradition of "burning sins."

In this ritual of fire, all of the sins that have been committed by an individual are written down upon a slip of parchment, which is then set on fire by the flame of a sacred candle blessed by a priest in the names of the Father, the Son, and the Holy Ghost. As the paper is reduced to ashes, so too are the person's sins, according to the old belief that echoes the rites of primitive sympathetic magick and offers but one more example of how many of the rituals of the Christian faith are rooted in, or heavily influenced by, the Old Religion of the Pagans. In some parts of the world, religious Catholics continue to practice sin-burning candle rituals.

Depending upon a practitioner's own preferences, candle magick rituals can be performed either indoors or outdoors. However, one important thing to take into consideration before setting up an outdoor altar is Mother Nature. Working out in an open area can have its drawbacks. A sudden gust of wind, a downpour of rain, and even the biting of bloodthirsty mosquitoes can be quite disadvantageous to a candle magick ritual. If stormy weather poses no threat and an outdoor ritual is desired, it is advisable to use glass-enclosed novena candles rather than tapers or pillars, which can easily be robbed of their flames by even the gentlest of balmy summer breezes. When practicing candle magick, the last thing you would want is for your carefully consecrated, blessed, and charged candles to suddenly be extinguished in the middle of a ritual. This would require bringing the ritual to a close and then starting over again from the very beginning.

Many Witches, myself included, always burn incense during candle magick rituals. An incense corresponding to the magickal working is always the best type to use, and you will find that many rituals call for a particular type of incense to be burned on the altar. In most cases when a specified incense cannot be obtained, a substitute can be employed with equal results—providing, of course, that it contains the same planetary, astrological, or elemental properties. Any form of incense—stick, cone, or the granulated type that is burned upon a hot charcoal block—can be used.

The fragrant rising smoke of burning incense aids concentration and fills a ritual space with mystical vibrations that help put a practitioner in a mood conducive to spellcasting. There is also an old Pagan belief that as the incense smoke rises upwards to the heavens, it carries a person's prayers and wishes to the gods and goddesses on high. However, the use of incense is in no way a strict requirement in candle magick. If a practitioner prefers not to burn incense because of an asthmatic or allergic condition or for any other reason, he or she should feel free to omit it from the ritual and proceed with the work at hand.

Dressing the Candle

Before any candle can be used in a candle magick ritual, it is important that it be properly "dressed." There are two very important steps in the dressing of a candle. The first step is to exorcise the candle of any negativity or previous magickal energy vibrations that may be embedded in it. This is traditionally accomplished by first casting a circle for protection and to create a sacred space, and then making the sign of the banishing pentagram in the air above the lit candle with the blade of an athame (a double-edged ritual dagger). Next, an incantation, such as the following, is thrice recited:

I call upon the flame to summon thee,
0 spirit of the fire.
I call upon the firedrakes and the salamanders
And all of the creatures who dwell within the
*   fiery realms*
To draw you into this circle.
Hear me, 0 spirit, hear me and rise.
Rise from the flickering flame and exorcise
This creature of wax and wick.
Let any and all negativity contained within it
Be now cast out!
Let any and all evils contained within it
Be driven out forthwith!
Let this creature of wax and wick
Be cleansed, sanctified, and blessed
For my intended purpose.
In the names of every god and goddess
To whom the flame is sacred,
I now consecrate this candle
As a tool of magick.
So mote it be!

The second step, after the exorcism and extinguishing of the candle's flame, is what is known as the "charging" or "loading" of the candle. It is not a complicated procedure, but it requires a great deal of concentration and visualization skills.

To charge a candle you must first select an essential oil appropriate for the magickal work at hand. For instance, if your candle ritual is concerned with affairs of the heart, you would use an oil that corresponds to love magick, such as rose, orris, clove, or jasmine. For a candle ritual to attract money, you would use oil such as bayberry, mint, pine, patchouli, or almond, and so forth. Three, seven, or nine drops of the essential oil, depending on what the particular spell calls for, are then poured onto the palm of your left hand. (Do not pour the oil directly onto the candle unless it is a glass-enclosed novena candle, in which case you would pour the oil onto the top of the candle and then, using the index and middle fingers of your power hand, rub the oil into the wax—clockwise to draw, or counterclockwise to banish.) Rub the palms of your hands together to warm the oil, and then concentrate upon your need or desire and visualize it in your mind's eye as you anoint the candle.

To draw something or someone to you, anoint the candle in the following manner: Rub the oil into the candle from the bottom end up towards the middle, and then from the wick end down towards the middle. If the candle ritual is intended to banish, then rub the oil into the candle from the middle down towards the bottom end, and then from the middle up towards the wick end.

Continue anointing the candle in this fashion until you sense that it has absorbed your vibrations. This may take a few minutes or longer. At this point, "seal" the candle by drawing the sign of the pentagram in the air above it, using the pointed index finger of your power hand or the blade of your athame. Close the ritual by giving thanks to the Powers That Be and then utter the words, "So mote it be!"

Types of Candles

Three types of candles are used in most candle magick rituals: a pair of altar candles, an astral candle, and one or more offertory candles.

Altar candles, which are sometimes called "invocational" candles, are placed at the left and right sides of the altar, and are always the first candles lit in candle magick rituals. Their flickering flames serve to invoke the divine presence of the Goddess and/or the Horned God (or any Pagan deity whom the practitioner wishes to invoke). White taper candles are most commonly used; however, some practitioners, especially those of the Wiccan traditions, prefer to use a black altar candle to represent the female aspect of the Divine and a white one to represent the male. Others use a silver and a gold altar candle, as the color silver corresponds to the Moon (symbol of the Goddess) and the color gold to the Sun (symbol of the God). Still other practitioners feel most comfortable employing a pair of altar candles of colors that correspond to the days of the week rather than to deities.

The traditional daily candle colors are as follows:

Sunday:	Gold or yellow
Monday:	Silver, gray, or white
Tuesday:	Red
Wednesday:	Purple
Thursday:	Blue
Friday:	Green
Saturday:	Black or purple

An *astral candle* represents the person for whom the candle-burning rite is being performed, whether it be yourself or someone else. Astral candles are burned only after the altar candles have been lit, and it is most important that their colors correspond to the astral (or zodiacal) colors of the person or persons at whom the spell is directed.

To determine a person's astral color, you may use the following chart (based on Raymond Buckland's *Practical Candleburning Rituals*) to match his or her zodiac sign to its corresponding primary and secondary colors:

Aries:	White; pink	Libra:	Black; blue
Taurus:	Red; yellow	Scorpio:	Brown; black
Gemini:	Red; blue	Sagittarius:	Gold; red
Cancer:	Green; brown	Capricorn:	Red; brown
Leo:	Red; green	Aquarius:	Blue; green
Virgo:	Gold; black	Pisces:	White; green

Other sources list different astral colors, such as red for Aries; orange or pink for Taurus; pale gray or yellow for Gemini; silver or pink for Cancer; gold for Leo; green or yellow for Virgo; lavender for Libra; red, burgundy, or indigo for Scorpio; yellow, orange, or green for Sagittarius; black for Capricorn; violet or dark blue for Aquarius; and white or purple for Pisces.

Conflicting color correspondences can be terribly confusing and frustrating, especially to an inexperienced spellcrafter who is new to the art of magick. My personal advice as a Witch who has been casting spells and working candle magick for close to 30 years is to listen to your heart and follow your own instincts when in doubt. Often it is best to simply choose your astral candle based on your personal favorite color, or one which you feel adequately represents you or corresponds to your current mood. Never burn an astral candle that is a color that inspires any strong negative emotions within you, even if your favorite Witch's spell book tells you that it is the correct color for your sign of the zodiac. What may suit the needs of one Witch may not always suit another's. It is a good rule of thumb to always work with what feels most right for you, even if it means bending the rules every now and then!

Some practitioners of candle magick mark their astral candles with the corresponding astrological symbol (see the following), along with the petitioner's name or initials and/or birthdate.

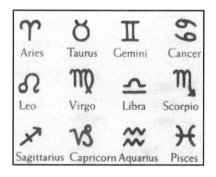

Those who follow the paths of Voodoo, Santeria, and Hoodoo folk magick commonly burn a glass-enclosed seven-day novena candle (available in many occult shops and botanicals) on their altars with a photograph of the person whom the candle represents placed in front of it.

An *offertory candle*, also known as the "purpose candle," is normally placed in front of the astral candle and is the last one lit during candle magick rituals. It is burned to represent the purpose of the ritual, and it is of the utmost importance that the color of its wax correctly correspond to the type of magick for which it is being used. For instance, a green candle would be appropriate for spells pertaining to money or fertility; a pink candle for drawing love, a red candle to arouse the flames of passion; a purple candle for spiritual healing or banishing evil, and so forth.

There is a wide selection of offertory candles to choose from, and nearly any type of candle can be used for representing the purpose of one's ritual. Glass-enclosed Novena candles are popular among many practitioners, as are seven-knob candles, double-action candles, triple action candles, separation candles, human image candles, and candles molded into the shape of skulls, devils, and black cats.

Once lit, *Novena candles* should be allowed to burn until their flames die out of their own accord. It is believed that extinguishing the flame of a Novena candle will abort your spell before it has been fixed. ("Novena" is a word of Latin origin, meaning "a new beginning." Many practitioners, therefore, make it a point to light a Novena candle when the Moon is new.) It is said that the lighting of a Novena candle yields positive results within the course of seven days.

A *seven-knob candle* is so named because it consists of a vertical row of seven round knobs of wax strung together with one wick. Traditionally, one knob of the candle is burned each day for seven consecutive days. White seven-knob candles are known as wish candles because each segment of the candle is burned daily as the practitioner concentrates upon the wish that he or she desires to be granted.

Double-action candles are also known as reversing candles because their main function is to reverse the evil effects of hexes

Glass enclosed Novena candles are popular among many
practitioners of candle magick. (Photo by Gerina Dunwich)

and curses. They are large candles of white, green, or red, which are half-coated in black wax from the middle down. It is believed that as the melting colored wax from the top half of the candle drips down and covers the black bottom half, the evil of a sorcerer's black magick becomes neutralized.

White and black *double-action candles* are ideal for reversing the effects of the evil eye, jinxes, and general hexes. Red and black ones work best in situations where black magick has been directed at your love life by a jealous or vengeful third party bent on destroying your relationship. In cases where the dark forces of black magick have been used to bring down a plague of financial woes upon your life to cause you misery and/or ruin, the burning of a green and black double-action candle is strongly recommended.

Tri-colored *triple-action candles* are and are commonly employed for banishing evil and negativity or bringing tranquility to a home that has been plagued by quarrels and hostility. The use of triple-action candles is particularly popular among practitioners from Latin America.

Separation candles are used to break up the relationships of others, reverse the effects of love spells, or free yourself from the emotional bondage to any man or woman who controls your heart. They are traditionally large red candles that are entirely covered by a coating of hand-dipped black wax. It is believed that as the outer coating of wax melts away to reveal the red portion underneath, the occult power of the candle begins to take effect.

Human image candles are molded into both male and female shapes and are available in various colors, most commonly black, white, red, and green. They are popular tools of Voodoo candle magick, and are used to inspire romantic feelings or intense sexual attraction between two people (when the two candles are placed upon the altar facing each other) or to bring about a separation (when they are placed back to back.) Human image candles are also used for healing, and their remains are traditionally buried in the Earth after the ritual has concluded, as per Pagan custom.

Skull-shaped candles are traditionally used in healing rituals, especially when the person in need of healing suffers from a serious or life-threatening illness. They are placed upon the altar next to the astral candle and then are moved about an inch apart from each other during each daily ritual.

According to an old occult belief, if the inner part of the skull candle melts away, but the face of the skull remains intact, this is a grave omen, portending the death of the ill person. In such a case, do not panic or abandon all hope. Repeat the candle burning ritual with a new skull candle and be sure to increase the amount of concentration and visualization you put into it.

Devil-shaped candles, also known as Satan candles, Diablo candles, or Devil-be-gone candles, are not used to summon forth the Prince of Darkness, despite their name. In fact, their function is quite to the contrary. They are burned on altars to exorcise all entities of a demonic nature, banish evil vibrations from a cursed or haunted house, and cure people believed to be demonically possessed. If the practitioner believes in the Devil and feels tormented by him, the burning of a Devil candle is said to help banish the Evil One from his or her life.

Wiccans and most Neo-Pagans do not believe in the Devil outside of the realm of symbolism, as the Devil is primarily connected to the Judeo-Christian and Islamic mythos, and not to Paganism (which predates all of the world's major religions). However, one does not need to believe in the existence of an actual Devil in order to accept the existence of evil or to benefit from the use of Devil candles. It cannot be denied that there are certain evil forces at work in the world, and it is naive and foolish to not believe that nearly all people possess the capability to commit acts of pure evil. Some individuals, such as Adolf Hitler and Charles Manson, for instance, appear to be innately evil. If a practitioner is confronted by evil in any form or manifestation and has strong faith that it will be banished as the waxen image of the Devil burns and diminishes, positive results can surely be obtained.

Black cat–candles have long been used by those whose lives have fallen victim to a streak of ill luck, whether it be through fate or deliberately induced by the Black Arts of another. It is believed that the action of the flame melting away the waxen image of the black cat (an animal which symbolizes bad luck to many folks, especially in the United States) magickally banishes the bad luck.

In candle magick rituals that are performed to bless a newborn kitten, heal a sick or injured cat, or ensure the safe return of a beloved feline friend or familiar to its home or covenstead, a candle molded into the shape of a cat can also serve as an astral candle to represent the cat. Cat-shaped candles are burned during all candle rituals of the Bast-Wicca tradition.

Parchments

Many practitioners of candle magick write out their needs or desires upon a piece of parchment paper, using a quill or fountain pen filled with either their own blood or a magickal ink such as dragon's blood or dove's blood, available in most occult shops and mail order companies that specialize in Witchcraft supplies. Traditionally, dragon's blood ink is used in spells concerning strength, power, domination over others, wealth, protection, uncrossing, binding, exorcism, and banishing. Dove's blood ink is traditionally used in spells concerning love, friendship, restoring emotional balance, legal matters, peace and tranquility, liberation, fertility, and travel. The parchment is then anointed with the same essential oil used in the dressing of the candles and placed beneath the offertory candles. At the end of the candle ritual, the paper is ignited by the flame of the offertory candle and placed in a fireproof container, such as an ashtray, incense burner, or small cast iron cauldron. The ashes of the burnt parchment paper are traditionally buried in the ground upon completion of the ritual, along with the remains of the altar, astral, and offertory candles.

In addition to, or in place of, the handwritten parchments of needs and desires, some practitioners place beneath their altars or astral candles parchments upon which are inscribed various magickal seals, occult symbols, talismanic designs, runic spells, incantational rhymes, prayers, magick squares, names of power, or veves, intricate symbolic emblems used to both represent and invoke the various Voodoo loas and saints. As with parchments, these too must be ritually anointed with the appropriate essential oil, burned at the end of the ritual, and then buried in the soil of Mother Earth.

Chapter 7

A Book of Shadows

Spells for the New Year

To ensure that your life is blessed with good luck throughout the next 12 months, perform this simple spell at the stroke of midnight on New Year's Eve. Open every door and window of your house to allow the spirit of the old year to depart. Go outside and light a green candle that has been anointed with a few drops of cinnamon, cypress, or lotus oil, and, without uttering a single word, reenter your house through the back door. Walk through every room with the candle in your hand, go back outside through the front door and then come in again through the back door. Additionally, you may also place a silver coin, a piece of coal, and a piece of bread on a windowsill or porch at midnight on New Year's Eve and then bring them into the house after you rise from bed on New Year's morning.

The following is a New Year's resolution spell.

Upon a square piece of parchment paper, write your New Year's resolution(s) using dragon's blood ink. Upon the paper, sprinkle a bit of dried mugwort, an herb ruled by the planet Venus and associated with strength, and then roll it into a tube and secure it in the center with a red ribbon. Anoint a new white candle with bergamot oil as you state your resolution(s) aloud. Light the candle with a match and then use its flaming wick to set fire to the rolled-up parchment. Cast the parchment into a small cast iron cauldron or other fireproof container and thrice recite the following incantation:

> *To the flames my words are spoken*
> *As the newborn year unfolds.*
> *Resolutions be not broken,*
> *Promises I shall uphold.*

A Ritual to Honor the Mother Goddess

Place a white, female-shaped candle at the center of your altar and arrange fresh flowers around it. This candle represents the Mother Goddess. Anoint it with three drops of frankincense and myrrh oil, and then light it with a match. After casting a circle and calling forth the guardians of the four Elements, gaze into the flame of the candle, raise your arms in a traditional Witches' prayer position with palms turned up, and say:

> *Mother Goddess, creatress most ancient,*
> *This Witch's circle is consecrated to Thee.*
> *You who are the giver of life...all that has been,*
> *   all that is, and all that will be.*
> *This candlelight ritual I do perform in Thy*
> *   honor.*
> *You are the eternal and infinite queen of the*
> *   gods and the greatest power on earth,*
> *She who commandest all that is the universe.*
> *Praise be to Thee, 0 Mother Goddess.*
> *So mote it be.*

Candlemas Spells and the Reading of Omens

Candlemas, which is called the Feast of Imbolc by Pagans of the Celtic traditions, is a time of year when many Witches celebrate change, which is equated with growth, and bid farewell to that which is no longer needed. Sweep the circle with a broom to symbolically sweep away the old in order to make room for the new and that which is yet to be born.

It is also a Pagan tradition to burn candles on this night as offerings to the Earth Mother so that her divine power of fertility may soon awaken from its long winter slumber and bring forth springtime. Light a green candle and thrice recite the following incantation:

> *Mother Earth, awaken from your silent Winter rest,*
> *Let thy springtime goddess of green magick manifest.*
> *Mother Earth, awaken now and hold us to thy breast.*
> *We honor thee with love for we are truly by thee blessed.*

Candlemas is also a traditional time for performing divinations pertaining to the new growing season and its weather, which is reflected in our relatively modern Groundhog Day, also celebrated on the second day of February. It is an old Pagan belief that the animals that come out of hibernation on Candlemas carry with them omens connected with winter. In the United States, if a groundhog emerges from its burrow on Candlemas and observes its own shadow, wintery weather is said to continue for another six weeks. In other regions of the world, if wolves return to their lairs on Candlemas, this portends at least another 40 days of winter ahead.

Beltane Anti-disease Spell

Beltane is an appropriate time to perform spells to ward off disease, as the ancient Celts once drove their livestock through the smoke of their sacred Beltane bonfires to keep diseases at bay.

To perform this spell you will need a piece of white chalk and a white candle that has never before been burned. With the chalk, draw a pentagram on the floor about 3 feet wide. Light the white candle and hold it in your right hand. Step into the pentagram, face the direction of East, and thrice recite the following incantation:

> *Beltane fire of enchantment,*
> *Burn without and burn within.*
> *Give this Sabbat spell enchantment,*
> *Let its power now begin!*
> *Ofano, oblamo, ospergo,*
> *Hola noa, massa lux beff,*
> *Clemati, adonai, cleona, florit,*
> *Pax sax sarax, afa afaca nostra,*
> *Cerum heaium, lada frium,*
> *So mote it be!*

Lammas Spells

The Sabbat of Lammas, which is also called Lughnasadh by Pagans of the Celtic traditions, is a Feast of Bread and a time when spirits and fairy-folk are believed to cross over into the human realm.

Corn Doll

An old Pagan custom associated with the first day of August is the making of a corn doll from the last sheaf of corn from a harvest. For good luck throughout the coming 12 months, the corn doll is traditionally hung up in the kitchen or on the chimney and kept there until the following Lammas, when it is ritually burned. It is said that if the previous year's corn doll is not removed before Christmas, the next harvest will be a poor one.

To make a traditional Witch's corn doll for good luck, twist or tie together into a small female figure a few stalks of corn. If desired, you may dress the corn doll and decorate it with dried flowers. Anoint it with a few drops of either frankincense or clove oil, and then pass it 12 times through the smoke of burning sage to consecrate it, as you chant your intent over it.

Bread Spells

For good luck and prosperity, bake a loaf of bread on Lammas and then cut the top of the loaf before cutting the bottom. This simple spell has been employed by Witches in both Scotland and England for centuries.

A piece of bread baked on Lammas and wrapped in an infant's bib or dress is said to work as a charm to protect the child from being stolen or from becoming the victim of evil or sorcery.

Sleeping with a crust of "holy bread" (panem benedictum) beneath your pillow is said "to keep Hags away." To keep a horse or other animal protected against thievery, according to the advice of a 15th-century English Witch, feed it holy bread and holy water. Holy bread blessed by the Lord's Prayer and marked with the symbol of a cross was once believed to work as a powerful healing charm for Christians and Pagans alike when placed on an afflicted part of the body.

A once common belief among sailors in England and other parts of the world was that vengeful Witches could bring about shipwrecks simply by turning a loaf of bread upside down on a table while muttering evil incantations. Laying a loaf the wrong side up is still regarded by some folks as a very unlucky thing to do.

Halloween Wishbone Divination

Halloween, which is called Samhain by Pagans of the Celtic traditions, has long been a traditional time of year for the reading of omens pertaining to affairs of the heart.

The following divination should be carried out at the witching hour on Halloween. To find out who will be the first to marry, two unmarried girls (or bachelors) must each take hold of a wishbone, close their eyes, and together break it into two pieces while saying:

> *Bone I wish the future read,*
> *Who shall be the first to wed?*

The girl who receives the bigger of the two pieces is portended to walk down the aisle before the other. However, spinsterhood is said to be destined for a girl whose wishbone slips from her hand during the working of the charm.

This old method of marriage divination is English in origin and dates back to the Middle Ages, and possibly before. Deriving from it is our popular American Thanksgiving custom of two people making a wish while breaking apart a wishbone, with the wish being granted to the one who ends up holding the bigger piece.

Hungarian Healing Spell

An old healing spell once used by Witches from Hungary called for an eggshell to be stuffed with the hair of a horse. It was believed that when the charm was rubbed on an afflicted part of the body, it would absorb the pain and disease. The eggshell, along with the infection, would then be cast into a blazing fire enchanted by the words of a now long-forgotten magickal incantation.

The Cherry Stone Love Spell

To attract a lover, an old Gypsy love spell instructs a young lady to gather 14 cherry stones (sacred to the goddess Venus). Each night, beginning with the first night of the new moon, she must drill a hole through one of the stones while stating her intent and visualizing the man of her desires (if there is one). On the 14th night, after drilling a hole through the last cherry stone, she must thread all 14 stones on a piece of red or pink thread and then hide the love charm in a secret place for a month. When the moon is once again new, she must take the threaded cherry stones and tie them around her left thigh or knee before going to bed and remove them the following morning upon rising. For the magick to be effective, this ritual must be repeated for 14 consecutive nights. According to old Gypsy lore, when the young lady's spell reaches its conclusion, a lover shall be drawn to her like a moth drawn to a flame.

A Love-Drawing Bath

To attract a new lover into your life, draw a bath during any of the Venus hours of Saint Valentine's Day. Add a handful of rose petals and six drops of musk oil to the bath water. (Six is a magickal number ruled by Venus.) To enhance the spell, love-attracting incense (such as African violet, cherry, cinnamon, gardenia, ginger, hibiscus, jasmine, lavender, lotus, rose, strawberry, or vanilla) may be burned. Surround the tub with the flickering flames of pink candles and then fill your mind with romantic thoughts as you bathe and recite the following incantation:

> *Lover hear me call to thee,*
> *Let these words enchant and draw.*
> *Lover find your way to me,*
> *Love is the magick, love is the law.*
> *As it is willed, so mote it be.*

Unfaithful Lovers

Most practitioners of Hoodoo folk magick are familiar with a magickal oil known as "Black Devil." Found in most occult shops and botanicas, this oil is used mainly by women whose lovers or husbands have been unfaithful to them. A few drops sprinkled on the man's clothing while he is sleeping will curse him with impotence if done with strong intent during a waning moon. However, if the man has remained faithful in the relationship, the curse of the Black Devil will have no adverse effect upon his manhood.

The Jade Dragon Spell

To dispel all negative vibrations and bad luck, place a small jade dragon upon your altar and anoint it with a few drops of cypress or lotus oil. Light some dragon's blood incense and place it in a fireproof burner to the right of the dragon. To the left of the dragon, light a new black candle that has also been anointed. Take the jade dragon in your hands and, as you concentrate upon your intent, pass it clockwise through the smoke of the incense nine times. (Nine is a highly magickal number, symbolizing completeness and the highest attainment of achievements on both a mental and a spiritual level.) After you have done this, return the dragon to the altar and recite the following incantation:

> *Let this dragon spell be made*
> *This hour to keep me safe from harm.*
> *Negative vibrations fade*
> *By power of the dragon's charm.*
> *So mote it be!*

Coffin Nails

Nails that have been removed from coffins are powerful instruments of magick and have long been highly prized by practitioners of the Black Arts. Driven through a photograph or a Voodoo doll fashioned in the image of an enemy, coffin nails are said to bring physical and/or mental torment, injury, or death to the intended victim. Some sorcerers deliver curses to their foes by sticking three coffin nails through the wax of a black candle that represents the flame of the victim's life.

In olden times it was common for many sorcerers to enlist the aid of a grave robber to unearth coffins in the dead of night and extract their nails. Nowadays such drastic measures are not necessary, for coffin nails are readily sold to the public in many occult shops and mail order cataloges.

A word of caution: Sorcery is an art that demands great respect and should never be approached in a frivolous manner, for there always exists a potential for dangerous repercussions to backfire upon the practitioner. The magickal use of coffin nails and other similar spells to inflict harm upon one's enemies should be resorted to only under extreme circumstances (such as matters of life and death) and when all else has failed.

The Enchantment of Herbs

Before any herb is used in spellwork, it should be properly enchanted to put its natural magickal energies in alignment with your own powers of will and intent. Some spellcrafters call this method charging or magnetization. But regardless of what you choose to label it, enchantment is a simple procedure that helps a spellcrafter achieve more favorable results. The act of charging an herb (or any other amulet or talisman) with emotional thought-force connects the spellcrafter to the power of the herb's magickal properties and helps to lay the groundwork for effective spellcasting. To sum it up in the words of the late Scott Cunningham, "The wise herbalist will never omit enchantments."

To enchant any herb, hold it in your power hand and directly in front of your eyes. Visualize your need or desire and direct it, along with your concentrated emotional feelings, like a power-beam into the herb. You may chant your intent in the form of a simple incantation if you find that this helps you to retain the image in your mind.

Continue projecting your thoughts and emotions into the herb until you feel both the herb and the tips of your fingers tingling with magickal power, similar to an electric current. This indicates that the enchantment is complete. The herb is now ready to be used in your spellwork.

A Spell to Attract Money

On a night when the moon is new or waxing and the planetary hour is in Jupiter, take a dollar bill (preferably one that bears the year of your birth) and, using dragon's blood ink, write upon it your money desire while focusing on your intent. Wrap the dollar bill around a pinecone and secure it with a piece of dark green yarn or ribbon. Anoint it with three drops of pine essential oil (or any money-attracting occult oil, such as Green Money, Money Drawing, or High John the Conqueror). If you were born under the astrological sign of the goat, use Capricorn Oil for maximum effectiveness.

Enchant the pinecone money charm by holding it between the palms of your hands and breathing the following incantation upon it:

> *This charm I fix,*
> *This spell I cast,*
> *In the mighty name of Bast,*
> *To make my wealth grow*
> *Like the moon during this time most*
> *   opportune.*
> *Work thee well now charm and verse*
> *To draw abundance to my purse.*
> *As it is willed, so mote it be!*

Bury the pinecone money charm in the ground without uttering a word. Using the blade of a consecrated athame or the extended index finger of your power hand, bring the spell to a close by drawing the symbol of the pentagram three times in the air over the buried charm.

A Witch's Cauldron Divination

There are a number of ways in which a cauldron can be used for divining. One method is to fill the cauldron with water or wine and place it between two burning candles or under the bright silver rays of the full moon. Relax, clear your mind of all distracting thoughts, and then gaze into the cauldron as you would a crystal ball. As with other forms of scrying, your vision will begin to blur after a while and a slight haze will begin to materialize. Keep your gaze focused, and eventually a vision, either of an actual or symbolic nature, may be revealed to you.

To determine good or bad omens according to an old Pagan method, place a cauldron upon the ground and within it burn some incense (traditionally frankincense) or a handful of dried herbs. Mugwort, rose petals, vervain, and yarrow are popular herbs of divination among many Witches. If the smoke rises straight up to the heavens, this indicates a good omen. If it does not rise or if it touches the ground, this indicates a bad one.

An old method of cauldron divination practiced by the Popoluca of Veracruz (Mexico) calls for a small ball of copal incense to be tossed into a cauldron of water while a question is being asked. If the incense floats, an affirmative answer is revealed. If it sinks to the bottom of the cauldron, the answer is a negative one.

Blood-Magick

Blood, both human and animal, has been used in spells since ancient times and "The Bloody Sacrifice" is without a doubt the oldest magickal rite known to mankind. The Romans were known to have consecrated their altars by sprinkling them with the blood of sacrificial animals, and the Celts, according to Tacitus, "deemed it indeed a duty to cover their altars with the blood of captives." Interestingly, the word "blessing" stems from the Old English bletsain, earlier bleodswean, which means "to sanctify with the shedding of blood."

A woman's menstrual blood (known as "moon blood" or "moon-dew" by the ancients) has long been prized as a highly magickal substance, possessing fertilizing and healing powers. In medieval times it was believed that menstrual blood could give birth to such demons as the basilisk, a serpentine creature whose glance deals death. Thessalian Witches were said to be able to poison their enemies with a girl's first menstrual blood shed during a lunar eclipse. According to fairy lore, there are certain elfin kings who can miraculously wake the dead from their sleep using a drop of moon blood, and an old Gypsy belief holds that a woman who brews a love philtre consisting of her own menstrual blood can romantically enslave the heart of any man who drinks it unknowingly.

Blood equals life. When blood is shed, according to magickal theory, the energy of life is released into the atmosphere. When the shedding of blood takes place within a magician's or Witch's circle, its energy can be caught and stored or redirected in the same manner that electric energy is harnessed and utilized.

The art and practice of blood-magick remains a rather controversial subject among contemporary Pagans (especially Wiccans), and not all spellcrafters feel comfortable incorporating blood into their magick. There is certainly no law, written or unwritten, that requires the use of blood in magickal workings. However, I have personally found that by pricking the tip of my thumb with a silver pin and adding a few drops of my own blood to a spell, greatly increases the potency of the magick in one way or another. I often add blood to potions, magickal inks, and candle anointing oils. But please note that I do not believe in using the blood of an animal for spellwork, nor do I condone the sacrificial slaughter of any living thing.

Spellcrafting in the Bast-Wicca Tradition

In 1999—appropriately the Year of the Cat in both Vietnamese and Chinese (Northern) astrology systems—I founded Bast-Wicca, which is open to all magickally minded individuals who hold a special place in their hearts for the cat. Named after the ancient Egyptian cat-headed goddess Bast, this tradition welcomes both male and female members, who are referred to as priests and priestesses, respectively. Those who function as leaders of covens are high priests and high priestesses.

Bast-Wicca is a Witchcraft tradition emphasizing the art and practice of feline magick. Combining elements of both High and Low Magick, it is based in part on the ancient religion and magickal system that centered around the goddess Bast in Egypt.

Bast-Wicca is not a cat-worshipping cult. Cats are regarded as sacred and created in the image of Mother Bast, but they are not idolized or worshipped as deities. Sacrificial rites involving cats, other animals, or humans are in no way connected to this tradition. Unlike many other Wiccan traditions, Bast-Wicca has no myth cycle of Goddess and God. Cord bindings and scourgings, which are common in traditions such as the Gardnerian and Alexandrian, are not practices associated with the Bast-Wicca tradition. The concept of threefold karmic return is not embraced. However, where the casting of spells is concerned, Bast-Wicca, like traditional Witchcraft, teaches that energy sent, whether positive or negative, equals energy returned to the sender. This occurs through the natural law of physics and is not connected in any way to the wrath of vengeful gods, angelic or demonic beings, or the mystical workings of karma. Incidentally, karma is a Hindu concept of fate and was never connected to the Old Religion of Witchcraft until Gerald Gardner incorporated it into his tradition of Wicca in the mid-20th century.

A Witch's altar dedicated to the ancient Egyptian cat-goddess Bast. Upon the altar sit a pair of red altar candles, a pentacle, an incense burner, an elaborate ritual dagger, and a cauldron guarded by two statues of Bast. (Photo by Gerina Dunwich)

The Bast-Wicca path teaches that all cats, regardless of color or breed, are highly psychic animals endowed with great magickal energies. Cats can aid a priest or priestess in divinatory rites, add more potency to spells and invocations, and protect against harmful spirits and Elementals both in and out of the ritual circle. All Witches who embrace the Bast-Wicca tradition have a spiritual, psychic, and magickal bond with one or more feline companions, known as familiars. Additionally, the spells, ceremonies, and divinations associated with this tradition are seldom performed without a familiar in attendance. (Felidomancy is the formal name for the art and practice of divination by the observation of a cat's behavior.)

The three great symbols of Bast-Wicca are the nine-pointed star (representing, among other things, the ninefold rebirth cycle of a cat's spirit), the Key of the Nile (also known as an ankh, the ancient Egyptian symbol of life), and the sun, which symbolizes Bast's original role as a solar deity. It was not until the arrival of Greek influence on Egyptian society that Bast became connected with the moon; Greeks associated her with their lunar deity Artemis.

Nine Lives

It is believed that cats (as well as other animals) possess both a spirit and a soul, and can experience rebirth just like their human counterparts. The rebirth cycle of a cat's spirit is ninefold, hence the old adage of a cat's "nine lives." After the ninth feline incarnation has been completed, a cat may then be reborn in human form. Sometimes cats remain in the spirit world and function as a familiar spirit guide for their human priest or priestess. It is also believed that in many cases a Witch is joined with the same cat-familiar in every lifetime. Such a spiritual bond may span hundreds or thousands of years.

Bast-Wicca Rituals and Customs

The birth of a kitten is a sacred event celebrated by a special Wiccan ceremony known as "kittening." This is a rite of blessing, which is often combined with a cat-naming ritual. In addition to a regular name, cats (like their human counterparts in the Craft) can also be given a secret Craft name known only by the cat's priestess, priest, or coven, and used only within the sphere of the ritual circle.

When a beloved familiar crosses over into the world of the dead, it is customary for the cat's body to be ritually perfumed with frankincense and myrrh, wrapped in a velvet or sacred cloth, and laid to rest in the soil of Mother Earth at the time of the witching hour (midnight). In keeping with ancient Egyptian tradition, the cat's human priest or priestess may completely shave off his or her eyebrows in order to show respect during the mourning period. This funerary custom was, at one time, observed by all devotees of the goddess Bast when their beloved cats were called away by death.

Bast-Wicca Sabbats

In Bast-Wicca there are three great Sabbats, celebrated each year on April 15, May 15, and November 16. Some priests and priestesses of the tradition also pay homage to Bast on October 31, which, in ancient times, was observed as the Feast of Sekhmet-Bast-Ra and is not related to Halloween and its Irish/Celtic roots. Five minor Sabbats are held each year: August 27, October 6, December 5, December 6, and December 14. (Note: These Gregorian calendar dates correspond to the dates of the ancient Bast festivals as they appeared on the old Egyptian calendar, according to *A Festival Calendar of the Ancient Egyptians.*) At these times, Bast invocations and honoring rites are performed, cat spells are cast, and omens are read. Additionally, there is feasting, drinking, dancing, and general merry-making.

Bast-Wicca Magick

As a deity originally associated with the rising sun, Bast is best invoked at dawn, when her energies are at their peak. It is also for this reason that all spells and rituals involving the invocation of Bast are believed to hold greater power when performed at sunrise during a planetary hour most favorable for the magickal working. Other spells and rituals may be performed at night, and lunar phases and astrological positions should always be taken into consideration. Spellcasting should never be done on days when solar eclipses occur, as these bring about unstable energies, which can be detrimental to the working of spells.

Cat-shaped candles are often burned in place of traditional altar candles, although this is more of a personal preference and not requisite to ritual work. Many Bast-Wicca altars can be found adorned with a cat's-eye (a gemstone that is a sacred charm to the cat-goddess and endowed with great magickal power), catnip (an herb beloved by all cats), and small statues of Bast and other cat figurines (winged cat angels and cat gargoyles are especially popular). Amulets bearing the divine image of Bast, as well as Bastet (as the cat-goddess is called when in her earthly form of a seated cat), can be worn by both priests and priestesses for magickal empowerment, protection, fertility, good luck, healing, and other purposes connected to the many attributes of Bast. Anointed with lotus oil, an oil sacred to the cat-goddess, Bast amulets can also be carried in charm bags and utilized in spells in various ways.

Not all spells and rituals require the goddess Bast to be invoked. However, a cat, in one form or another, should be incorporated into all spells and rituals, regardless of the intent behind them. This can range from having a cat-familiar present in the circle during the casting of the spell to working magick with such cat charms as fur, whiskers, claws, and so on.

On the Bast-Wicca path, all cats—regardless of color or breed—are regarded as sacred animals. (The Hulton Picture Library)

Chapter 8

Fertility Magick

Fertility Folklore

L
ong before modern Witches chanted spells to win hearts, secure pay raises, or safeguard journeys, spellcasting was concerned primarily with the fertility of humans, animals, and the land. Fertility magick in its earliest forms was simplistic, consisting of such practices as painting images on the walls of caves, eating or smoking certain plants believed to be endowed with magickal qualities, ritual dancing and other symbolic bodily gestures, and reciting of special words or phrases believed to possess mystical power.

In pre-Christian times, it was believed that eating fish on a Friday would ensure fertility in women. The reason for this was that fish were sacred to the Greek and Roman love deities, Aphrodite and Venus, respectively, and that Friday (the most favorable day of the week for fertility magick) was under the rulership of the goddess Venus. Thus the Catholic tradition of eating fish on a Friday is one with undeniable Pagan roots, despite the fact that this will probably never be admitted by the Church.

The frog (sacred to Venus and a symbol of the fetus in ancient Egypt) has been connected to fertility magick since antiquity. To cure women of barrenness and to protect those who were with child from miscarriage, the Babylonians employed special cylinder seals showing nine frogs as a powerful charm. It is believed that the number nine is significant as it relates to the Ninefold Goddess, who rules over the nine months of human gestation.

Herbs have long played an important role in fertility magick, being employed as natural amulets and also as ingredients in cauldron brews designed to promote fertility in both human and beast, as well as in the body of Mother Earth. According to *Cunningham's Encyclopedia of Magical Herbs,* the following plants possess, or were at one time believed to possess, the power to magickally increase fertility: agaric, banana, bistort, bodhi tree, carrot, cuckoo-flower, cucumber, cyclamen, daffodil, date palm, dock, fig, geranium (especially the white-flowered varieties), grape, hawthorn, hazel, horsetail grass, mandrake, mistletoe, mustard, myrtle, nuts, oak, olive, patchouli, peach, pine, pomegranate, poppy, rice, sunflower, and wheat.

The fig tree (sacred to the Pagan deities Dionysus, Isis, and Juno) has been used in a number of ways to promote fertility. Its wood is carved into small phallic images, which are carried by females to ensure conception and by men to maintain male sexual potency or overcome impotence and sterility. The fruit of the fig tree is believed to work powerful fertility magick when eaten between the hours of 4:30 and 7:30 a.m. when the Moon is waxing or full. (In the Northern Tradition, these three hours are the "tides of day" corresponding to fertility, as well as to arousal, awakening, and vitality, according to Nigel Pennick's *The Pagan Book of Days.)*

Eating olives (which are sacred to the Pagan deities Apollo, Athena, Irene, Minerva, and Ra) or carrots, as well as carrying an acorn, a pinecone, a bit of dragonwort (an old folkname for the bistort), or any type of nut are said to be effective forms of magick to increase fertility and strengthen sexual potency.

Ruled by the planet Venus, the cuckoo-flower is utilized in many spells for lovers as well as in fertility magick. To promote conception, a woman is advised to carry a tuber from the cuckoo-flower. If a male child is desired, she must carry a large tuber. If a female child is desired, she must carry one that is small.

Seeds have long been regarded as possessing great power to bestow fertility. Eating any of the following seeds is said to make a barren woman fertile: carrot, cucumber (ironically, eating the fruit is said to hinder lust), pomegranate, poppy, and sunflower. Of course the mere act of eating a seed cannot, in itself, guarantee fertility. In order to be truly effective, the spell must be carried out on the first night of the waxing moon and then repeated each night thereafter until Lady Luna reaches her fullness. Additionally, the seeds must be properly consecrated and enchanted before being eaten, and, as with any magickal operation, the entire process must be done with intent clearly stated and the end result visualized.

The popular custom of throwing rice over a bride and her groom for good luck as they leave the church after their wedding ceremony is actually the remnant of a pre-Christian fertility rite. After a Pagan couple were handfasted, special incantations would be recited and rice would then be cast into the air above them as a magickal gesture to increase the couple's fertility. It was believed that the more rice that was thrown, the greater the couple's chance for producing a large family.

This custom in turn stemmed from an even older Greek fertility rite of showering a bride and groom with sweetmeats, which also served to confer prosperity on the newlyweds. Over the centuries the true meaning and origin of the rice-throwing custom faded; however, the custom itself never died out and remains with us in the present day.

Spells to ensure the fertility of the soil and promote a bountiful harvest in the coming year have been practiced since early times by farmers in nearly all parts of the world. Placing a hen's egg or a loaf from the previous year's harvest beneath the plow before cutting the first furrow was a simple method popular in Western Europe, and in Ireland a sickle would be placed in the center of a corn field "as a reminder to the crop of its eventual destiny."

Farmers in Italy at one time scattered poppy seeds throughout their cornfields to promote growth by flower-magick. The poppy was a plant sacred to Ceres, a Roman goddess of the Earth and its fruits, who was once viewed as the source of all food. Farmers believed beyond the shadow of a doubt that if they were not faithful in keeping her rites they would be cursed with crop failure.

Witch's Milk

A rather curious fertility spell from olden times called for the drinking of what was known as "Witch's milk," a thick, sweetish secretion produced by the tiny swollen breasts of certain male infants. This powerful elixir was highly prized by Witches for its alleged magickal potency. It was said to cure not only infertility in humans, but numerous sex-related problems as well.

In an unenlightened age when the unusual or unexplained almost always was equated with sorcery or the supernatural, breast milk in male infants naturally came to be regarded as an extremely magickal substance and it was not uncommon for midwives to "milk" baby boys for the precious fluid. However, there is hardly anything supernatural about "Witch's milk." For the first few days after a baby boy is born, his breasts, which are glands, are influenced by his mother's potent mix of hormones. When his breasts are squeezed (which is not recommended by doctors), milk flow is stimulated. The swelling of the breasts and production of milk lasts for approximately one week and does not pose any threat to the health of the child.

Pagan Fertility Deities

Since ancient times, mankind has called upon the gods for their protection, guidance, and favors. And in just about every known pantheon there can be found deities, both male and female, who govern all aspects of fertility.

When the ancient Egyptians called upon the divine to empower their fertility rites, they invoked deities such as Osiris, Ba, Min, Hapy, Sarapis, the cow-goddess Bat, and the snake-goddesses Amaunet and Renenutet. The fertility of the Celts was governed by deities such as Cernunnos (the Horned One), Brigit, Epona, and Macha. In the Scandinavian region the fertility gods were known as Disir, Fjorgyn, Freya, Frey, Nanna, and Vanir. The pantheon of the early Mesopotamians was abundant with fertility deities, the most popular of these being Baba, Dumuzi, Inana, and Ishtar. Xochiquetzal was a popular and beloved goddess among Aztec women, who invoked her to ensure that their marriages would be fruitful.

Other well-known fertility deities throughout the world include, but are not limited to, Demeter, Adonis, Kronos, and Priapos (Greek); Abundantia, Ceres, Egeria, Fauna, and Faunus (Roman); Astaroth, Astarte, Baal, Kades, Myrrha, Quades, Sulmanitu, and Ugar (Western Semitic); Anaitis (Persian); Aphrodisias (Turkish); Attis (Phrygian); Eostre (Anglo-Saxon); Nerthus (Danish); Obatala (Nigerian); Saraddevi (Buddhist-Lamaist); Sauska (Hittite and Hurrian); Venda (Indian); Wamala

(African); Zemyna (Lithuanian); and Astoreth (Palestinian and Philistine).

Easter Fertility Spell

Easter, named after the Anglo-Saxon fertility goddess Eostre, is an appropriate time for the casting of spells to ensure fertility. At midnight on the eve of Easter, take a hard-boiled egg that has been dyed green with food coloring, and, by the light of a green candle, write upon it your name and draw the astrological symbols that correspond to the time of your birth. As you do this, concentrate upon your intent and say:

> *I enchant this egg, symbol of fertility,*
> *Sacred to the goddess Eostre,*
> *To be a charm to work for me.*
> *With fertility my body it shall bless,*
> *By the powers of the Earth,*
> *The seas, the winds,*
> *And the flames of fire.*
> *So mote it be.*

Place the egg under your pillow and then lay yourself down to sleep. At the first hour of sunrise, take the egg outside and bury it in the earth.

A Candle Spell for Fertility

The following magick was inspired by a fertility spell published in the *Tides of Illumination* newsletter, volume 1, issue 1, Imbolc/Ostara 2000.

To aid in the conception of a child, perform the following spell when the moon is either waxing or full. Press nine cloves into the base or sides of a newly purchased, or newly crafted, green candle. As you do this, visualize your intent. Anoint the candle with three drops of your own menstrual blood. Hold the candle to your belly and then recite the following incantation nine times:

By magick spell a seed I sow,
Within my womb let new life grow!

Place the candle upon an altar beneath the rays of the moon and light its wick with a match. As its flame dances, recite the following incantation nine times:

By power of the mother goddess,
By power of her sacred name,
By power of the silver moon,
By power of the candle's flame,
A seed I sow, a seed I sow,
Within my womb let new life grow!
Harming none, this spell is done.
As it is willed, so mote it be!

Allow the candle to burn out. If you need to extinguish the candle before the spell has been completed, pinch out the flame with your moistened fingertips or use a candle snuffer. Do not use your breath to blow out the flame. When the candle is relit, again repeat the ninefold incantation. Take the remains of the candle and bury it, along with a seed of any type, in the fertile soil of Mother Earth. When the seed sprouts, the magick of your spell will begin to take effect.

Chapter 9

Weatherworking

Weatherworking is a type of spellcasting designed to bring about changes in meteorological patterns, most commonly to conjure forth rain or wind and to make them cease. Ritual dances, the tying of knots, chanting, and the reciting of special incantations are but several examples of weather magick practiced the world over by Witches and other spellcasters since the earliest of times.

The use of magick to control the weather is mentioned in *History of the Persian Wars,* which was written by a 5th-century Greek historian by the name of Herodotus. In this ancient work the author writes, "But, at length the Magi, having sacrificed victims and endeavored to charm the winds by incantations, and moreover, having offered sacrifices to Thetis [a sea-goddess] and the Nereids [female spirits or nymphs of the sea], laid the storm on the fourth day."

The chanting of the old and well-known children's rhyme, "Rain, rain, go away. Come again another day," and its variations is actually a derivative of weatherworking in its most simplistic form. Beneath its innocent exterior, it echoes the ancient occult belief in the power of spoken words to bring about changes in nature.

Hanging a dead frog in an orchard or a vineyard is said to keep a fog at bay, and an old Finnish spell to banish mists called for a sword to be plunged into the water of a lake in order to make the fog ascend to the heavens.

Siberian shamans believed that ritually urinating on the naked body of a woman could induce rain to fall. Apparently the shaman's urine represented the "golden rain" of the sky god, and the female body represented the Earth goddess.

Even more bizarre was the ancient Eleusinian custom of offering the severed genitals of a male sacrificial victim to the goddess of fertility in exchange for rain. Eventually such human sacrifices were outlawed, and ritual offerings of serpents and phallus-shaped loaves of bread were made in place of the actual phallus.

Top: A male Witch sells wind tied in knots to seafarers.
Bottom: Witches use magick to raise a storm at sea.
(16th-century woodcuts by Olaus Magnus)

Magicians of the Malay Peninsula in Southeast Asia are said to be adept in the ancient art of weatherworking. To summon the wind, they chant the following invocation:

> *Come hither, Sir,*
> *Come hither, my Lord,*
> *Let down your locks so long and flowing.*

To quiet a storm, the following Malay pawang (Witch doctor) charm is believed to possess great magickal potency:

> *Though the stem of the Meranti tree rocks to*
> *   and fro,*
> *Let the Fam leaves be as thick as possible,*
> *That rain and tempest may come to naught.*

According to demonologist Francesco Guazzo in his *Compendium Maleficarum* (first published in 1608), "Witches can control not only rain and hail and wind but even lightning with God's permission." A rather interesting statement, considering that it was published during the Burning Times, when Church officials were busy brainwashing the masses into believing that all actions of Witches were sanctioned by God's enemy, the Devil.

The following plants, when dried and then burned in outdoor fires, are believed to possess the power to summon rain: bracken, cotton, ferns, and heather. Throwing rice into the air and picking pansies early in the day when the dew still clings to their leaves are also regarded as means of rainmaking through the innate magickal powers of plants.

Herbal sorcery can also be used to summon the winds, as the following examples demonstrate: Throw cuttings of the broom plant (also known as besom) into the air while invoking the sylphs, the Elemental spirits of Air. This spell is said to be especially effective if a Witch performs it while standing on the summit of a mountain or the top of a very high hill. To calm the wind, a Witch is advised to burn the broom and place its ashes into a small hole dug in the ground, which should then be filled in with soil.

The ancients of Persia employed saffron in a number of ways to raise and control the wind, and Witches in many coastal regions throughout the world found that standing on the shore and whipping a long strand of seaweed in a clockwise manner above their heads while whistling very softly was effective in raising a breeze. However, a Witch who possessed the power to do this had to take care not to whistle too loudly for fear of "whistling up" a gale.

The casting of a coin (especially a penny or a sixpence) or a brush into the waves of the sea while invoking Father Neptune is said to call up the wind, as does scratching the mast of a ship with a fingernail or sticking a sharp knife into it (the latter being an old method popular among sailors from the Shetland Islands.)

Seafarers often carry a piece of beryl as a charm to ensure a favorable breeze, and at one time it was common for Witches to sell winds to sailors in the form of a handkerchief, or a length of string or rope with three knots tied in it. Undoing the first knot conjured up a good sailing breeze. Undoing the second knot conjured up a strong gale, and undoing the third brought a severe tempest or hurricane.

In the 12th century, Sumner wrote in *Last Will and Testament,* "In Ireland and in Denmark both, Witches for gold will sell a man a wind, which in the corner of a napkin wrapp'd, shall blow him safe unto what coast he will."

Many Witches in the Middle Ages were believed to have made a fine living selling fair winds to those who were port-bound, and in the April 7, 1902 edition of the *Irish Times* a story was published about an old Witch by the name of Bessie Millle. As late as the year 1814, she was known to have sold magickal "wind-knots" to seamen at the price of "6d a vessel."

Weatherworking women were generally well-respected and their unusual services in high demand. Wise sailors were careful not to set a Witch's ire to blaze, for they knew all too well from seafaring legends that women (as well as men) who were skilled in the arts of spellcasting could easily raise a storm at sea fierce enough to send any ship and its crew to a watery grave.

Magickally induced storms, like as with other weather phenomena, eventually dissipated on their own accord after running their course. Or, for a Witch's price, they could be laid to rest by the same magick that was responsible for their creation.

In Austria, Witches wishing to stop a storm would throw a handful of coarsely-ground grain out of an open window and speak a charm. Storms were once believed to have been caused by angry spirits, and such a meal served as an offering to sufficiently appease them.

A particularly unusual method to banish rain comes from jolly old England. It requires the firstborn child of a family to undress and then stand on his or her head while uttering the words of a magickal rhyme. The reasoning behind this procedure is not entirely clear, but it must have yielded results at one time (or, at the very least, have been believed to be effective), or it would not have been recorded.

In the British Isles during the Middle Ages, a number of occult beliefs and practices were connected to rainbows. A rainbow arched over a house was thought to be an omen that death would soon pay a visit to the family that dwelled within, according to *Shetland Lore*. This superstition is probably rooted in the Old Norse myth of the celestial bridge over which the dead (particularly children) cross to get to Heaven. Stepping upon a miniature "rainbow" in an oily patch on a wet road is supposed to invite bad luck, but holding your foot above it and intoning, "Rainbow, rainbow, bring me luck. If you don't, I'll break you up" brings good luck. Pointing a finger at a rainbow in the sky is said to be a most unlucky thing to do, and sometimes it causes the rain to return.

A spell known as "crossing out" was once used to drive away a rainbow or negate its evil influence, according to the book *A Dictionary of Superstitions*. The recipe to dispel the multicolored sign in the heavens is as follows: Using two sticks or straws, make a cross on the ground and then lay four pebbles on it, one at each end of the cross. This was once a popular tradition among children in England.

Weatherworking in the Name of God

Historically, weatherworking was not an art confined only to the ranks of Witches, shamans, or other Pagan practitioners of magick. In fact, many centuries ago weather spells were commonly employed by many Christians and even by the Church itself. Several examples are as follows:

To stop a hail storm from wreaking havoc upon the land, the *Malleus Maleficarum* (a 15th-century Witch hunter's handbook) offered the following spell:

> *I adjure you, hailstorms and winds,*
> *By the five wounds of Christ,*
> *And by the three nails which pierced His hands*
>   *and feet,*
> *And by the four Holy Evangelists, Matthew,*
> *Mark, Luke, and John,*
> *That you be dissolved and fall as rain.*

Casting three hailstones into a roaring fire while thrice reciting the Lord's Prayer and the Angelic Salutation was another method once used by the Church to halt a hailstorm and, at the same time, bring torment to the Devil. The weatherworker then had to recite the Gospel of Saint John while making the sign of the cross in each of the four directions before bringing the ritual to a close by saying, "By the words of this Gospel may this tempest be stopped."

Church officials in the early centuries of Christianity believed that tempests (violent windstorms) were caused by storm-demons dispatched by Satan. They further believed that by ringing their church bells they could drive away these minions of the Devil, thus averting the adverse weather. Prayers, sacraments, and the invocation of the name of the Lord were all believed to offer the faithful blessed immunity against storms and tempests.

An old weatherworking charm, popular among many Christian farmers and sanctioned by the Church, called for flowers to first be consecrated on Palm Sunday and then placed in fields to safeguard the crops from Mother Nature's seasonal inclemency.

In times of drought, Christians in Europe once resorted to dipping crosses or other religious relics in holy water as a means to encourage rainfall. This practice undoubtedly stemmed from an even older Christian custom, that involved dipping statues of the saints in the water of rivers and lakes as a petition to the heavens to send forth a drought-ending downpour.

The curious relationship between weatherworking magick and the early Christian Church is summed up rather nicely by this passage in Rosemary Ellen Guiley's *The Encyclopedia of Witches and Witchcraft*:

> *"The medieval Church prohibited superstitious remedies against Witchcraft, such as storm raising, because of their Pagan associations. What the Church recommended, however, was little more than superstition with a sacrament thrown in, and rituals that replaced magic incantations with Christian ones. In essence, they were Pagan remedies trussed up with Christian window dressing."*

The Witch Broom Rain Spell

An old Witch's spell to make rain calls for the bristles of a broom to be dipped into a bucket of cold water (preferably rainwater). With broom in hand, face the direction of East and give the wet bristles a shake. Visualize rain clouds gathering and drops of rain falling from the heavens above. As you do this, recite the following incantation:

> *Clouds of the East*
> *Now heed my call,*
> *Bring thy rain*
> *And let it fall!*

Turn to the direction of South. Give the broom another shake and call upon the clouds of the South:

> *Clouds of the South*
> *Now heed my call,*
> *Bring thy rain*
> *And let it fall!*

Turn to the direction of West. Give the broom another shake and call upon the clouds of the West:

> *Clouds of the West*
> *Now heed my call,*
> *Bring thy rain*
> *And let it fall!*

Turn to the direction of North. Give the broom another shake and call upon the clouds of the North:

> *Clouds of the North*
> *Now heed my call,*
> *Bring thy rain*
> *And let it fall!*

Turn full circle back to the direction of East. Holding the broomstick horizontally in both hands, raise your arms to the sky and repeat the following rhyme:

> *Rain come hither*
> *I decree!*
> *As it is willed,*
> *So mote it be!*

To Turn Away a Storm

To turn away a storm, place a pair of scissors in the middle of your garden with the sharp end pointing upward to the sky.

Visualize the clouds clearing or moving in a direction away from you while you thrice recite the following incantation over the scissors:

> *Thunder, lightning, wind, and rain,*
> *By this spell be now restrained.*
> *Change thy course away from me,*
> *As I will it, it shall be!*

Chapter 10

A Kitchen Witch's Miscellanea

I t does not require a great deal of time, energy, or money to transform an ordinary kitchen into a magickal workplace. To begin with, there are many simple yet effective charms, such as a rope of garlic, a sun-catcher, or pentagram symbols, that can be placed in the kitchen for protection. Hanging a "Kitchen Witch" doll in your kitchen is said to attract good luck, and drawing an invisible pentagram inside your pots and pans with a wand or athame before using them adds magick to your cooking. A wooden spoon, fork, or knife can also be used for this purpose.

A sunny kitchen windowsill filled with potted plants not only decorates the kitchen but also releases magickal energies into the room. Even the most common culinary herbs found in the cupboards of nearly every kitchen possess strong magickal properties. For instance, basil is traditionally used for exorcism, love spells, protection against evil, and purification. Parsley is used for fertility, protection, and inspiring passion between lovers; sage is used for healing, protection, and prosperity; and thyme is used for clairvoyance, spells to increase one's courage, and spells of an amatory nature. Other kitchen herbs and spices attract good fairies and repel the bad ones, keep ghosts and demons at bay, act as a magnet for good luck, and bring pleasant dreams, to name just a few examples. For further information, see the complete listing of herbs and spices and their traditional magickal uses at the end of this chapter.

For best results, talk to your plants daily, using a gentle and loving tone of voice. Treat them, and yourself, to some mellow music whenever you get the chance. Studies have shown that plants respond well to music, especially New Age, Jazz, and Classical varieties. In fact, in some cases music therapy has been known to work wonders for ailing plants. On the other hand, some music (such as loud heavy metal and rap music) causes plants to wither and eventually die after long exposure.

Be sure to plant, care for, and harvest all of your herbs—whether they are grown for magickal purposes or strictly for culinary use—in accordance with the simple rules of the old Pagan tradition of gardening by the signs and phases of the moon. (For complete information on lunar gardening, see my book, *The Wicca Garden*, Citadel Press, 1996.) Lunar gardening is by no means foolish superstition or old wives' tales. I firmly believe in the positive and negative influences that the moon exerts over all plants, as well as all other living things. And having found greater gardening success by working in harmony with the lunar cycles instead of working against them, I can personally attest to the validity of this old agricultural tradition that Pagan country folk have known about for centuries.

A well-stocked Witch's kitchen should not only contain herbs, but also essential oils, a mortar and pestle, candles of various colors, different types of incense, an up-to-date lunar calendar, and a cauldron for brewing potions. Smudge your kitchen with a sage bundle if you sense negativity. Anoint utensils and appliances with essential oils to bless and charge them with powerful vibrations. Always stir food in a clockwise direction, and be sure to invite the Goddess and Her consort into your new magickal workplace.

A Witch's Kitchen Blessing

Blessed be this kitchen
Of Air, Fire, Water, and Earth.
Be warmed by the sacred light
Of the Goddess and the Horned one.
May all that is created here by means both
    magickal and mundane
Bring nourishment, healing,
And sustenance;
And cause harm to none.
With love and peace,
With joy and magick,
Be now and always filled.
So mote it be!

Kitchen Deities

Throughout the world, many cultures have believed in, and worshipped, various kitchen gods and goddesses. These deities are generally regarded as benevolent, and their presence is said to offer protection against kitchen accidents, fires, and food poisoning; to keep negativity, ghosts, and evil influences out of the kitchen; and to bless all foods that are prepared.

The Hindu god Annamurti, a form of the god Vishnu, is the patron deity of kitchens and food. Offerings of payasa (sweetened milk and rice) are traditionally placed before his bronze image at his shrine in southern India.

In Japan, the god and goddess of kitchens are Oki-Tsu-Hiko-No-Kami and his consort, Oki-Tsu-Hime-No-Kami. They are the children of the harvest god, and their main duty is to look after the cauldron in which water is boiled. Another Japanese deity associated with the kitchen is Hettsui-No-Kami. She is the goddess of the kitchen range. Each year on November 8 she is honored in Japan with a Shinto festival called the Fuiqo Matsuri.

The Chinese god of the stove was a deity who was greatly respected, for he possessed the power to bestow a family with good health, wealth, and prosperity. To keep him from being offended, all family members would take great care not to sing, swear, cry, or kiss in front of the stove. To chop onions on or near the stove was also regarded as disrespectful and was forbidden.

The Four Elements

In addition to the Pagan gods and goddesses of the kitchen, the spirits of the four ancient Elements are strongly connected to, and make their presence well-known in, the Witch's kitchen.

The refrigerator is an appliance dedicated to Air. This Element is also linked to the steam given off by hot foods and boiling liquids. Fire, the source of heat and symbol of transformation, dwells within stove and hearth. Water rules over the kitchen sink as well as the liquids used in the preparation and cooking of foods and potions. Vegetables, fruits, nuts, herbs and spices, and even meats and poultry, are all gifts from our blessed planetary Mother. These foods, which nourish and sustain us are, of course, ruled by the Earth Element.

The Elemental spirits of Air, Fire, Water, and Earth can be invoked at any time in the kitchen for protection, empowerment, magickal aid, and so forth. It is through the use of these four basic Elements that kitchen magick is created.

Kitchen Omens and Superstitions

The reading of omens is an art and practice dating back to antiquity. Omens reveal many things and can be found all around us, if we permit ourselves to be aware of them. They can be quite beneficial, especially in warning us of dangerous situations. The trick is to know how to correctly interpret the omen. The kitchen is one place in which many omens manifest. For instance, a rainstorm is portended by the repeated boiling over of a coffeepot, and also by the accidental spilling of water on a tablecloth. Money will soon be coming your way if any of the following things should occur: bubbles appear in a cup of coffee, you accidentally knock over a sugar bowl, rice forms a ring around the edge of a pot, or tea leaves float to the top of the cup.

In many houses and apartments, the back door is located in the kitchen. According to superstition, it is very unlucky to enter by this door when moving into a new residence or when returning home from a marriage ceremony.

Trouble is indicated by the accidental omission of spices from a recipe or by the spilling of salt. And be prepared for an argument with someone if you should happen to spill pepper on the kitchen table or floor. (According to occult tradition, these bad omens can be remedied by simply adding the spices, and by tossing a pinch of salt or pepper over your left shoulder, respectively.) It is also said that if two persons stir the same boiling pot or sit together on a table, they will soon find themselves involved in a quarrel.

If your apron "comes untied of itself" and falls off while you are working in the kitchen, this is generally seen as a sign that someone is thinking about you. Some say that it means your sweetheart is having romantic thoughts about you at that moment. It is believed by many to be an omen of good news when baked apples burst while in the oven or when salt and sugar are accidentally mixed up.

If a fork accidentally falls onto the floor, a woman will soon knock on your door; a spoon indicates the arrival of a gentleman. (In some parts of the world, the fork means a man and the spoon a woman.) Unexpected or unwelcome visitors are also presaged by the dropping of a knife that sticks in the ground and by cracks that form on the shells of eggs boiling in a pot of water. To avoid bad luck, never place a billhook upon the kitchen table. And if you are engaged or wish to get married, according to an old belief once common in England, you should take care to never sit on a kitchen table, for this will break the engagement and also prevent you from ever being wed.

There are also numerous kitchen omens concerning bread. It is considered unlucky in certain countries to wash a bread knife on a Sunday, cut both ends of a loaf of bread, leave a knife stuck in the loaf, or take the last slice of bread. Accidentally dropping a slice of bread with the buttered side down is also said to be a bad omen; however, it is a good sign if the dropped bread lands with the buttered side up. If you and another person reach for the same slice of bread at the same time, an unexpected visitor will soon be paying you a visit.

Magickal Uses of Everyday Kitchen Items

Broom

Brooms, sacred to the goddess Hecate and one of the most powerful symbols of Witchcraft, can be used in spells and rituals in place of a wand as they were in centuries past. In Europe during the Witch-burning era of the Inquisition, women who practiced the magickal arts of the Old Religion needed to take every precaution against arousing the suspicion of those looking to find incriminating evidence of Witchcraft. It was well-known that in most cases suspicion led to arrest, prosecution, torture, and the inevitable execution. Because broomsticks were a mainstay of every kitchen, many a clever Witch used them as a safe substitute for a magick wand.

A broom's handle can be carved or painted with magickal and/or astrological symbols, runic names or monograms, and so on. Additionally, crystals and other magickal gemstones, amulets, and talismans can be attached to it with bonding adhesive.

Before casting a spell or commencing with a ritual, sweep the circle with a broom to symbolically sweep away any and all negative vibrations and evil spirits from your sacred space. Brooms, especially ones fashioned from the broom plant, can also aid a Witch in the practice of weatherworking magick. (For more information on this, see Chapter 9.)

Throwing a broomstick into the air has long been regarded as a simple yet powerful act of magick to bring good luck. It is also believed to ward off all harm caused by those who dabble in black magick. If a man or woman was believed to be under the influence of sorcery, an old remedy from Scotland called for a broom to be thrown on him or her. This was supposed to be quite effective in breaking any type of bewitchment. Animals that were believed to have been bewitched were cured in the same fashion.

To safeguard your home against intrusion by sorcerers, according to an old English custom, lay a broom across your door-way. This simple act is said to prevent any man or woman whose heart is black with sorcery from entering your abode and doing you harm. *Lancashire Legends* (first published in 1873) adds that with a broom placed across the threshold, a sorcerer who comes to the door "will make an excuse and pass along the road."

Numerous superstitions have long been connected to brooms. In England there is a saying that "brooms bought in May sweep the family away." It is said to be equally unlucky to buy a broom during the 12 days of Christmas. An unmarried girl who steps over a broomstick will find herself to be a mother before a wife. Setting a broom in a corner invites the visit of a stranger to your house. Sweeping the top of a table with a broom brings bad luck, as does laying a broom upon a table. To ensure good luck, always rest a broom on its handle and never on its bristles.

One of the oldest, and perhaps the most popular, superstitions surrounding broomsticks is that they can be made to fly when enchanted by Witches with a special flying ointment. This belief, which originated in the Middle Ages, was widespread throughout Europe and New England. Of Witches and broomsticks, Oldham wrote, "So witches some enchanted wand bestride, and think they through the airy regions ride."

In ancient times, country Witches were known to use brooms when performing fertility rites to induce the growth of their crops. Mounting their broomsticks and riding them like hobby horses through the fields, they would dance and leap high into the air while uttering magickal charms. Some Witchcraft historians theorize that this broomstick "fertility dance" of Witches was the origin of the popular cultural stereotype of the broomstick-riding Witch.

The broom, the cat, and the moon are three symbols that have been linked to Witches since the ancient times. (The Hulton Picture Library)

Knife

An ordinary kitchen knife (or letter opener) can function as a Witch's ritual dagger (also known as an athame) as long as it is ritually cleansed and purified, personally charged with energy, and consecrated prior to use.

To personalize your dagger and make it more magickal, you can carve upon its handle (if wooden) the sign of the pentagram (a five-pointed star within a circle), the symbol of your astrological sign, your Craft name in runes, or whatever magickal symbols you prefer. You can also engrave these upon the blade with an engraving tool or etch them by either using an etching pen (available at most hardware stores) or by using a sharpened nail to inscribe them upon a beeswax-covered blade, which is then treated with an etching agent such as iodine or sulphuric acid. After several minutes, the blade is rinsed under running water to wash off the iodine or acid, and then the beeswax is removed.

Be careful when working with etching agents because they can be dangerous, and it is always a good idea to practice first on a piece of scrap metal or an old knife that can be discarded until you get the hang of it. For more information on creating magickal knives and marking in metal, read *Buckland's Complete Book of Witchcraft* by Raymond Buckland (Llewellyn Publications).

Knives have long been used by practitioners of the Black Arts. When given to a couple as a gift, a knife of silver is sure to sever the thread of love. The same is said to be true of scissors. To bring misfortune to one who has done you harm, lay two knives or a knife and a fork crosswise over his or her picture. To cause a quarrel between two people, put their pictures together, face-to-face, and then lay two crossed knives upon them. To break the spell, uncross the knives, tap each handle three times upon a wooden table top, and then throw the knives onto the floor as you say:

> *Knives uncrossed,*
> *Spell be tossed!*

In Victorian times it was popular among many practitioners of the occult to foretell events of the future by spinning a knife around on the top of a table. Numerous methods were connected to this form of divination, such as predicting the hair color of a future wife or husband (dark-haired if the spinning knife stops with its blade pointing towards you; light-haired if the blade points away from you), determining from those seated at the table who would be the first to marry, the first to have children, the first to die, and so forth.

To spell out messages (often in the form of anagrams), spin a knife clockwise in the center of a circle marked with letters of the alphabet and/or numbers, and record each letter or number the tip of the blade points to when the knife comes to rest. A knife spun in the center of a circle of rune stones is another way to manifest a divinatory message from the gods, the spirit world, or the clairvoyant realms of your own mind.

Salt

Salt has long been used by Witches as an agent of purification and to ward off negativity, evil vibrations, and foul spirits.

Symbolizing the Element of Earth, salt is a staple in the magickal arts and Pagan religious worship. In the tradition of Wicca, consecrated salt, along with water, flame, and incense, is used to consecrate the circle and the various tools of spellcraft.

In medieval times it was widely believed that salt possessed the power to render demons and evil ghosts impotent. For this reason, necromancers were known to avoid eating food containing any salt prior to performing rites to call forth the spirits of the dead.

Sprinkling salt in the cradles of infant children was once done as a precaution against demonic possession of the newborn, and salt sprinkled in a coffin assured the dead person's protection against soul-snatching demons. To prevent an unwanted visitor from returning to your house, sprinkle some salt on the doorstep as he or she leaves, sweep it up with a broom, and then cast the salt into a fire. Throwing a pinch of salt at the back of departing visitors is another method that is supposed to keep them away for a long time, if not permanently.

For good luck to come into your life, throw a pinch of salt over your left shoulder thrice, each time saying:

> _Bad luck turn_
> _And bad luck flee._
> _Good luck fortune_
> _Come to me!_

To release a victim from the influence of the evil eye, many Witches in Scotland would use a borrowed sixpence to scoop up a bit of salt, which would then be put into a tablespoon of warm water. After the salt dissolved, the sixpence would be put into the solution. Three times the soles of the curse-afflicted person's feet, the palms of his hands, and the tip of his tongue would be anointed with the saltwater. The healing Witch would then dip her finger into the saltwater and draw it along the brow of the patient. After doing this, the contents of the spoon would be cast "into the hinder part of the fire" and the Witch would cry, "Lord and Lady preserve us frae a' scathe [harm]!"

To break any spell of sorcery that has been cast over you, perform the following counter-spell at sunrise for nine days in a row: With your right hand, sprinkle some salt into the dancing flames of a fire as you thrice recite these words:

> *Salt! Salt! I cast thee to the flames.*
> *Now may the person who has bewitched me*
> *Neither eat, drink, nor find peaceful rest*
> *Until the spell is broken!*

Sprinkling salt into a fire on seven consecutive mornings is said to make an absent lover return, and wearing a salt-filled charm bag under a wedding gown brings good luck to a bride and ensures a happy marriage. To make a vision of your future husband or wife appear before you, throw a pinch of salt into the fire at the witching hour on three Friday nights in succession. As you do this, repeat the following incantation:

> *It is not this salt I mean to burn,*
> *But my true loves heart I mean to turn.*
> *That he (or she) may know no rest or glee,*
> *Until he (or she) comes and speaks to me.*

There exists a widespread superstition that spilling salt brings a person bad luck. Whether or not there is any truth to this is impossible to say; however, there is certainly no harm in taking precautions. Negate the impending bad luck by immediately tossing a pinch of salt over your left shoulder with your right hand while saying:

> *With this cast,*
> *May bad luck pass!*

Pots and pans

Ordinary cooking pots can often be used in place of cauldrons in spells and divinations. Be sure not to use any pots that are coated with Teflon if you intend to burn herbs, incense, or rubbing alcohol in them.

To make a scrying tool: When the moon is new, take an old pot and paint the inside of it black. If you desire, you may paint or engrave astrological and/or magickal symbols on the outside of the pot when the moon is full (and it is even better if it is also positioned in the astrological sign of Pisces), fill the pot with water or oil, and then gaze into it by the soft glowing light of a candle until visions appear in your mind's eye. If you are new to the art of scrying, do not become discouraged if you are unsuccessful at it in the beginning. Like any other art, scrying requires practice and patience before it can be mastered.

Earthenware pots are said to be able to predict how many years of happiness a couple will enjoy together: When the moon is full, take an earthenware pot in your hands, close your eyes, and concentrate intently upon your lover for at least one hour. Now release your grip on the pot and allow it to fall to the ground and break. Count how many broken pieces it made and this shall tell you the number of years.

Long ago it was a common custom among Pagan folk to cast seven grains of salt into the fire before hanging a pot above a hearth. This was done to drive away evil spirits. It is said that to avoid a quarrel, two cooks should never stir the same pot and strangers should never be allowed to lift the lid from a pot boiling on the fire. Another old superstition, and certainly a curious one, holds that if an unmarried woman should wipe the bottom of a pan with a piece of bread, wedding bells will never ring for her.

The Magickal Properties of Culinary Herbs and Spices

Allspice

Ruled by the planet Mars and the Element of Fire, allspice is used in magickal spells designed to promote the healing of body, mind, and spirit. To make a healing tea good for colds, menstrual cramps, or an upset stomach, add one or two teaspoons of all-spice powder to one cup of boiling water when the planetary hour corresponds to Mars. Allow the tea to steep for 10 minutes. Before straining and drinking, stir the brew clockwise with an iron utensil as you enchant it by visualizing your magickal intent (which, in this. case would be healing) while thrice repeating the following magickal incantation:

> *In the name of Mars and in his hour,*
> *This brew I enchant with healing power.*
> *So mote it be!*

To spice up a Sabbat celebration, add half a dozen allspice berries in a punch bowl filled with mulled wine or hot apple cider.

Many modern day Witches and practitioners of the magickal arts burn allspice during a waxing moon whenever good luck or money is needed, for this spice has long been valued in the spellcasting community for its alleged magickal power to overcome bad luck as well as poverty. Allspice is an ingredient commonly added to many money-attracting incense mixtures.

Anise

Ruled by the planet Jupiter and the Element of Air, anise is used as both an herb and a spice. The leaves (herb) have long been used to keep evil at bay, and in the Middle Ages many practitioners of ceremonial magick would arrange the leaves of the anise around their magick circles in the belief that they offered protection against demons and hostile spirits. According to folklore, if a man or woman sleeps with a sprig of anise hung on the bedpost, he or she will forever remain young. Anise is also said to hold the power to restore lost youth.

Anise seeds (spice) are often used in incenses that are burned for protection against evil supernatural forces, to aid meditation, and to conjure forth spirits of the dead. In some parts of the world, anise seeds are believed to render the malevolent glance of the evil eye powerless. Many Witches keep their slumbers free of unpleasant dreams by sleeping with a small mojo bag filled with anise seeds beneath their pillows. Anise seeds, along with leaves from the evergreen bay tree, are often added to the water of purification baths, which are traditionally called for prior to many magickal rituals

Basil

Ruled by the planet Mars and the Element of Fire, basil has been used in the arts of love magick and love divination since ancient times. If a betrothed woman wished to know if her future marriage held happiness or sorrow for her, all she needed to do was place two fresh basil leaves together upon a hot coal and then observe their reactions. If they burned quietly and quickly to ashes, this was a sign of a happy marriage. If the leaves crackled fiercely as they burned, this indicated a quarrelsome husband. If they crackled and then flew apart, this was an unlucky omen, indicating that the marriage would end in a bitter divorce.

To find out if your lover has been true to you, place a sprig of fresh basil in the palm of his or her hand when the moon is full. If your lover has been untrue, the basil will instantly wither before your very eyes, according to an old legend.

Basil is also used in spells to increase wealth, keep evil at bay, exorcise ghosts and demons from haunted places and possessed persons, and attract good luck. In olden times it was believed in some parts of Europe that sorcerers could work black magick with basil to make poisonous scorpions materialize out of thin air! Many people also believed that Witches (especially female ones) brewed potions from the juice of the plant which, when consumed, enabled them to mount a broomstick and take to the night sky.

Bay

Ruled by the Sun and the Element of Fire, the bay is an herb that was once used by the priestesses of Apollo to magickally induce prophetic visions. To look into the future through dreams, sleep with bay laurel leaves beneath your pillow.

The following divination, according to *Aristotle's Last Legacy*, must be performed on the eve of Saint Valentine's Day and, if it is carried out correctly, will induce a dream in which a vison of one's future marriage mate will appear: "Take two Bay-leaves, sprinkle them with Rose-water; the Evening of this Day, lay them a cross under your Pillow, when you go to Bed, putting on a clean Shift, and turning it wrong side outwards; and lying down, say: Good Valentine, be kind to me, In dreams let me my true Love see. So crossing your Legs, and go to sleep...you will see in a Dream the Party you are to Marry."

The bay has long been used for protection and purification. Wearing a mojo bag filled with bay leaves keeps bad luck and evil forces at bay and prevents the wearer from being struck by lightning, and hanging one in a window is said to deter lightning from striking the house. "He who carrieth a bay-leaf shall never take harm from thunder" is an old English proverb, and in Thomas Lupton's 16th-century work, *A Thousand Notable Things of Sundry Sortes,* it is written that "Neyther falling sickness, neyther deuyll, (devil) wyll infect or hurt one in that place: wheras a Bay tree is. The Romaynes calles it the Plant of the good Angell."

The burning of bay leaves, in combination with words of power, works well to exorcise ghosts and demons from haunted dwellings and the possessed. When combined with sandalwood and burned when the moon is on the wane, bay laurel leaves break the most evil of curses. Burning a bay leaf upon which a wish has been written in your own blood is believed to make manifest that which you so desire.

Capers

Ruled by the planet Venus and the Element of Water, capers (the flowering buds of the caper bush) are used in various ways in the art of love enchantment. Some Witches use them to stuff poppets representing the man or woman at whom a love spell is directed. Others enchant the spice by spoken charm and visualization and then add it to the food of the person whose affections are desired. Capers are said to induce intense feelings of lust, and at one time it was believed that if an impotent man added capers to his daily diet, his "lost manhood" would in time be fully restored.

Caraway

Ruled by the planet Mercury and the Element of Air, the seeds of the caraway plant have been used in rituals of magick since ancient times. Many Hebrews believed that caraway seeds were effective amulets against the blood-drinking she-demon known as Lilith. No spirit that dwells in darkness can bring harm to a man or woman who carries caraway.

Many love enchantments from olden times call for caraway seeds. To draw love to you, wear or carry a pink or red mojo bag filled with caraway seeds and fail not to anoint the bag with three drops of rose oil every Friday when the planetary hour favors Venus. According to occult folklore, to win the heart of another you must chew caraway seeds while thinking of the man or woman who is the object of your desires. Another way to win a heart is to serve to your beloved a cookie, a piece of cake, or a slice of bread into which enchanted caraway seeds have been baked. If you are successful in enchanting the seeds by spoken charm and visualization, the heart of your beloved will beat with love only for you after he or she eats the offering.

Caraway seeds are also said to encourage fidelity, guard children against illness, strengthen mental powers and the memory, and keep thieves at bay.

Catnip

Ruled by the planet Venus and the Element of Water, catnip is found in the kitchen cupboards of many Witches with cats as familiars or members of the family. In addition to creating a psychic bond between feline and human, catnip is an excellent herb to use for love enchantment. Fill a red or pink sachet with equal parts catnip, rose petals, and lavender. Enchant it by spoken charm and visualization, and then give it to the man or woman whose affections you desire.

Not only does catnip work well to attract love, but it attracts good luck and beneficial spirits as well. For these reasons, many Witches and other magickally inclined folks grow catnip in their gardens and in other areas around their homes. When hung over the door and windows, catnip leaves and flowers are said to keep bad luck from entering. As the magickal attributes of catnip are influenced by the Roman goddess Venus, who presides over beauty in addition to affairs of the heart, this herb works well in any spell cast for the enhancement of beauty—both inner and outer. Another use for catnip leaves, as suggested by Wiccan author Scott Cunningham in *Cunningham's Encyclopedia of Magical Herbs*, is to press the large ones and use them as bookmarks in your grimoires.

Chamomile

Ruled by the Sun and the Element of Water, chamomile is said to be an herb possessing protective qualities. If you feel that a curse or enchantment has been cast upon you, sprinkling chamomile clockwise around the perimeters of your property when the moon is on the wane will help to counter the magick. A tea brewed from chamomile flowers helps to calm the nerves and induce pleasant dreams.

Cinnamon

Ruled by the Sun and the Element of Fire, cinnamon is added to sachets and potions and burned as an incense in spells to attract money, heal sickness, facilitate clairvoyance, and protect against the evil intentions or negative energies of others.

To magickally induce lusty feelings in a certain man, take a red phallus candle upon which his name has been inscribed and anoint it with three drops of cinnamon oil blended with your sexual fluids while visualizing the outcome of the spell. After the candle has been anointed, light its wick, have faith in your magick, and wait for the spell to take effect.

Cloves

Ruled by the planet Jupiter and the Element of Fire, cloves are commonly burned by Witches as a magickal incense to exorcise ghosts, purify a ritual space of evil and vibrations of negativity, draw love, attract money, and put an end to malicious gossip. Cast cloves into a bonfire or a cauldron filled with flames, or grind cloves into a powder using a mortar and pestle, and then sprinkle them over a hot charcoal block in an incense burner.

Cumin

Ruled by the planet Mars and the Element of Fire, cumin (a seed of a plant in the parsley family) is used by Witches to keep evil at bay and to exorcise ghosts from haunted dwellings. This spice is also used in love magick to induce feelings of lust in another person and to keep one's lover from being untrue.

Cumin seed has long been regarded as a possessor of the "gift of retention." What this means is that any object that retains cumin seed is magickally safeguarded against theft by man, spirit, or Elemental. According to German folklore, bread into which cumin seeds have been baked cannot be stolen by the fairies.

Dill

Ruled by the planet Mercury and the element of Fire, dill has long been regarded as an herb of protection. It has been used for many centuries as an herbal amulet to ward off sorcery, break hexes, and keep demons and malevolent spirits at bay. It is said that fairies will not come near a house or a garden where dill grows.

To prevent enemies from entering your home, according to an old Pagan custom, hang a charm bag filled with dill over your front door. To keep children safe as they sleep and dream, place a dill-filled charm bag in their cradles or beds.

Garlic

Ruled by the planet Mars and the Element of Fire, garlic has long been used as an amulet to protect against such things as evil spirits, blood-thirsty vampires, robbers and thieves, enemies, sorcerers, Mother Nature's furies, and disease. It was once a common seafaring custom to keep garlic on board ship to prevent disasters at sea. Carry cloves of garlic in a mojo bag to keep unlucky influences from jinxing you.

Garlic is sacred to the goddess Hecate. Each year at midnight on the 13th day of August (the Pagan Festival of Hecate) many Witches throughout the world gather at crossroads to celebrate their rites and to leave garlic as sacrificial offerings in Hecate's name.

An old Irish custom to draw good luck is to plant cloves of wild garlic on thatch over the front door. In Scotland, when the veil between the worlds of the living and the dead grows thin on Samhain and myriads of phantoms and specters roam the dark shadows of the night, garlic is hung throughout houses (especially over all doors and windows) to keep evil-natured spirits from entering.

Ginger

Ruled by the planet Mars and the Element of Fire, ginger has long been used in spells to attract money. One magickal method calls for a gingerroot to be dried in the sun for nine days and then ground into a powder with a mortar and pestle. When the waxing moon is in the sign of Taurus, visualize the outcome of your spell while sprinkling your pockets with the ginger. If your magick is worked properly, with gold and silver shall they soon be filled.

It is a tradition among some Witches and other practitioners of the magickal arts to eat a bit of ginger prior to spellcasting in order to add more potency to their magick. In addition to drawing money and adding extra power to spellwork, ginger is often used in working rituals to promote health, increase an individual's psychic powers, attain success, and lay curses against enemies when the act of cursing is justified.

Mace

Ruled by the planet Mercury and the Element of Air, mace is a spice derived from the red skin that surrounds the nutmeg seed. If you wish to increase your psychic powers, take some mace, either ground or whole, and burn it on a hot charcoal block as a magickal incense when the moon is in a waxing phase and in the astrological sign of Pisces or Scorpio.

Marjoram

Ruled by the planet Mercury and the Element of Air, marjoram works as a natural amulet for protection against evil, and is an herb associated with the ancient art of love enchantment. To help win the love of the man or woman of whom you are desirous, add a pinch of marjoram to his or her food while visualizing the outcome of your spell, and then serve it to your intended. For maximum effectiveness, be sure to work your love enchantment during a planetary hour of Venus on a Friday when the moon is waxing. If your timing is just right and your will is strong, amatory success shall be yours!

Mint

Ruled by the planet Mercury and the Element of Air, mint possesses protective healing properties and is used by many Witches to purify a ritual space of evil spirits and all bad vibrations.

To conjure the presence of beneficial spirits to assist you in your magickal endeavors, place one or more sprigs of fresh mint upon your altar prior to spellcasting. For the healing of stomach ailments, some Witches recommend stuffing a green poppet with

mint leaves and ritually anointing it with any occult oil designed
for healing purposes.

Mustard

Ruled by the planet Mars and the Element of Fire, mustard
seeds are traditionally used in protective magick. To keep evil
spirits, negative influences, and sorcery from invading your home,
an old spell from Italy calls for mustard seeds to be sprinkled on
the threshold of your doors and the sills of all your windows.
Carrying a mojo bag filled with mustard seed offers additional
protection, especially when one ventures far from the safety of
his or her home.

Nutmeg

Ruled by the planet Jupiter and the Element of Fire,
nutmeg is a spice long reputed to attract good luck and ward off
illness. Carrying nutmeg in your pocket is an old remedy for lum-
bago and rheumatism. To cure a boil, according to an old method
used by Witches in Europe, a male patient must be given nutmeg
by a female, and vice versa. The patient must then place the nutmeg in his or her pocket, taking it out every now and then to
nibble off a little bit of it. As the nutmeg gradually decreases in
its size, so too shall the boil, until it has disappeared completely.

To increase your wealth, sprinkle a pinch of ground nutmeg
onto a green candle and then burn it when the moon is waxing
and in the astrological sign of Taurus. According to some Gypsies, sprinkling a bit of powdered nutmeg on a lottery ticket and
leaving it undisturbed for a day and a night will add luck to its
numbers and increase its chances of winning.

The following spell, if performed correctly, will keep the one
you love from becoming unfaithful to you: With the blade of your
consecrated athame, quarter a nutmeg. Offer one piece to Mother
Earth, one piece to the winds, and one piece to the Element of
Fire. Boil the remaining piece in a cauldron filled with water and

then, after it has cooled, partake of the water and keep the piece of nutmeg with you at all times as an amulet.

Oregano

Ruled by the planet Venus and the Element of Air, oregano is an herb that possesses the power to protect against evil, sorcery, and negativity. When planted around a house, it keeps both the dwelling and those who inhabit it safeguarded from ghosts, curses, and jinxes. Some Witches use oregano in spells to draw love, and others use it in working rituals involving animals, grieving, harmony, peace, and psychic development. When mixed with violets and carried in a mojo bag, oregano is said to work as an amulet to ward off colds.

Parsley

Ruled by the planet Mercury and the Element of Air, parsley is an herb with a background rich in superstition and Pagan lore. Among Witches, the most popular magickal use of parsley is as an herbal amulet for protection against bad luck, evil influences, enemies, and black magick.

According to English Folklore, if a young woman sows parsley seed, she will soon find herself with child. However, a woman who desires motherhood should refrain from eating parsley, for consumption of this herb is believed by some to prevent conception. A 17th-century spell to induce an abortion calls for a sprig of parsley to be inserted "into the Mouth of the Womb, and it will presently cause the Child to come away, tho' it be dead, and the after-burden also."

In olden times it was believed by many superstitious Christians that parsley was an herb of the Devil (hence its folk name, "devil's oatmeal") and that only those of a wicked nature could grow it in their gardens with ease. It was also said of parsley that its seeds must be sown nine times before they sprout and that they go to the Devil nine times before coming up.

Pepper

Ruled by the planet Mars and the Element of Fire, pepper is said to be the most commonly used spice in the world. Amulets to which pepper has been added are thought to protect those who wear them from harm caused by jealous rivals and foes, and to render powerless those who possess the power of the evil eye. When mixed with salt, pepper can also be used in exorcism rites to dispel the powers of evil, cast out demons, and banish ghosts.

Poppy Seeds

Ruled by the Moon and the Element of Water, poppy seeds (as well as the flowers of the poppy plant) are traditionally used in spells and rituals for drawing love, increasing wealth, attracting good luck, and promoting fertility. According to occult lore, drinking wine in which poppy seeds have soaked for 15 days will give an individual the power of invisibility.

Saffron

Ruled by the Sun and the Element of Fire, saffron was once used in the weatherworking magick of the ancient Peruvians to summon forth the wind. Many contemporary Witches have been known to use saffron in healing spells and in the art of love enchantment. An infusion of saffron, prepared and drunk when the moon is full and in the astrological sign of Pisces, is said to induce psychic visions of the future.

Sage

Ruled by the planet Jupiter and the Element of Air, Sage has long been valued by practitioners of the magickal arts as an herb of purification, exorcism, and protection. Sage (often combined with cedar) is traditionally made into "smudging wands" and burned by shamans to dispel negative vibrations and evil spirits from a ritual space, to attract beneficial spirits, to "cleanse" the chakras, and for protection before engaging in rituals or trance-work.

Sage is also used in healings, money spells, and wish-magick. A small horn filled with sage is a powerful amulet of protection against the evil eye. Carrying a mojo bag filled with sage helps to promote wisdom, and eating sage every day throughout the month of May is said to ensure a long life. Bad luck befalls those who plant sage in their own garden, according to an old superstition. Therefore, a stranger should always be employed to do the planting.

According to Charlotte Sophia Burne in *Shropshire Folk-Lore*, sage can be used to divine the future in the following manner: "On All Saints' Eve, a young woman must go out into the garden alone at midnight, and while the clock strikes twelve she must pluck nine sage-leaves, one at every stroke up to the ninth. Then, if she is destined to be married, she will see the face of her future husband; if not, she will see a coffin."

Sesame Seeds

Ruled by the Sun and the Element of Fire, sesame seeds are said to "possess the powers to discover hidden treasures, reveal secret passageways, and open locked doors," according to *Cunningham's Encyclopedia of Magical Herbs*. Many Witches and other practitioners of the magickal arts use the seeds of the sesame plant in spells to increase wealth. Fill a small cauldron with sesame seeds when the moon begins to wax and leave it, with the lid off, in your house to draw money.

Spearmint

Ruled by the planet Venus and the Element of Water, spearmint is also known by the folk name "Our Lady's Mint," which reflects the plant's association with the goddess Venus (although some Christians would argue that "Our Lady" is a reference to the Virgin Mary.) Witches have long used the fragrant leaves of the spearmint and its plant in healings and protective magick. Dream pillows stuffed with spearmint are said to protect sleepers against attacks of sorcery, nightmares, and evil entities of the night, such as the incubus and succubus demons.

Tarragon

Ruled by the planet Mars and the Element of Fire, tarragon is traditionally used in spells and rituals involving commanding others, confidence, courage, passion, protection, and strength. This herb has long been associated with mythical dragons and ancient serpent-goddesses, and its name derives from the Greek word *drakon*, which means dragon.

In the Middle Ages, pilgrims were known to place sprigs of tarragon in their shoes before embarking on a journey in the belief that the herb would help to keep them safe from accidents, wild animals, robbers, evil spirits, and the Devil in his many guises.

Thyme

Ruled by the planet Venus and the Element of Water, thyme is often burned as a magickal incense or smudge to promote healing, attract good health, and cleanse a ritual area of any and all evil forces and negative vibrations prior to magickal workings.

When placed beneath the pillow, thyme is said to prevent nightmares. And, according to herbal lore, when thyme is worn it strengthens psychic powers and bestows upon the wearer the gift of fairy-vision (the ability to see fairy folk, who are normally invisible to the human eye).

Turmeric

Ruled by the planet Mars and the Element of Fire, turmeric is traditionally used by Witches and other practitioners of the magickal arts in the following types of spellwork: commanding others, confidence, courage, exorcism, passion, sensuality, spell-breaking, and strength.

In the Hawaiian Islands, where turmeric is known as olena, the herb was once used in the purification rites of the kahunas, initiated practitioners of an ancient esoteric tradition known as Huna, or the Hidden Knowledge. In a hollowed-out coconut shell or a skull, turmeric would be mixed together with the salty water of the sea and then, with a leaf, sprinkled upon the altar and throughout the ritual space to dispel evil spirits and negative vibrations.

Chapter 11

Yuletide Witches, Superstitions, and Spells

Yule, one of the four lesser or minor Witches' Sabbats, takes place each year on the Winter Solstice, which occurs on or about December 21. The old date of the Winter Solstice was December 25 (the birthday of the Persian god of light, Mithra, and other Pagan deities), which the Roman Catholic Church adopted as Jesus Christ's birthday in the early 4th century. Traced back to an ancient Norse solstice festival, it originally marked the rebirth of the Sun God from the Earth Mother.

Kris Kringle is thought by some to be the god of Yule; however, in the Nordic countries Yule is celebrated in honor of the Pagan god Frey. In pre-Christian France, a phallic deity whose phallus was symbolized by the Noel log was believed to have presided over Yule. This deity, who was similar in many ways to the Celtic Cernunnos, was often invoked in rites of fertility magick.

In parts of Europe and the British Isles, the Yule log symbolized a horned Pagan deity known as the Green Man, and its ashes were believed to possess magickal fertilizing powers. This belief gave birth to the old custom of scattering Yule log ashes like sacred seed on the soil of Mother Earth to ensure a bountiful harvest in the coming year. Traditionally, ashes from the Yule log were also used as a charm to safeguard houses against lightning, and they were mixed with cow fodder to help them calve or to rid them of vermin.

In the myth cycle of certain traditions of Wicca, each year on Yule a deity known as the Oak King (lord of the waxing year) takes the place of the Holly King (lord of the waning year, who bears a resemblance to our modern Santa Claus.) He reigns supreme until the Summer Solstice, when the Holy King once again reclaims his throne. It is believed that these two kings are in some way connected with the Druids, to whom the holly and the oak were highly sacred.

On December 25, according to German folklore, a Yuletide Witch known as the Lutzelfrau flies through the sky on her broom, bringing mischief to mortals who fail to honor her with small presents. Another Yuletide Witch of German folklore is Perchta. In the southern regions of the country, it was an old Yuletide custom for children wearing masks and carrying besoms to go door to door (in trick-or-treat fashion) begging for gifts in the name of Perchta.

Yuletide Superstitions

Yuletide is a festive season and the most popular time of the year for many people throughout the world. It is governed by a wealth of Pagan traditions and centuries-old superstitions.

Animals were said to be able to speak in human voices each year when the clock struck midnight on Christmas morning. Also at the witching hour on this night of the year, divinatory voices could be heard at dark and deserted crossroads (sacred to the goddess Hecate), and water in wells and springs (sacred to Brigit and Coventina, the Mother of the Covens) could miraculously transform into either blood or wine.

Curious superstitions connected to the Yule log abound. It was once regarded as extremely unlucky to burn one in the presence of a cross-eyed person or a woman who was barefooted or flat-footed. It was also said to be unlucky to disturb a burning Yule log during supper on Christmas Eve. To ensure good luck over the following 12 months, according to folklore, a piece of burned Yule log should be placed under the bed. Supposedly, this also protects a house against lightning and fires.

Holly, ivy, and mistletoe, three plants traditionally associated with the Yuletide season, sacred to the Druids, and linked to old Pagan folklore, should never be brought into the house prior to Christmas Eve. According to this superstition, which can be traced back to England in the Middle Ages, to do so invites bad luck into your house. Additionally, these three plants should be kept in the house only until the morning after Twelfth Night and then burned. To throw them out or destroy them in any other way is said to conjure the worst of ill luck.

Nearly everyone is familiar with the old Yuletide custom of kissing beneath the mistletoe for good luck (a relic of the ancient Druidic fertility rites), but it is also said that if a girl marries without ever kissing under the mistletoe, she will be unable to bear children. Another old superstitious belief connected to the mistletoe is that if mistletoe decorations are not burned on Twelfth Night, all of the couples who kissed beneath it will end up quarreling before the year is through.

In England, Yule candles were popular in the 19th century and were traditionally lit on the eve of Yule and allowed to burn all night. The superstitious believed that failing to burn a Yule candle or lamp on this night invited the Angel of Death into the house. Many folks also believed that Yule candles brought good luck only if they were given as gifts and not bought for oneself. It was considered unlucky to light a Yule candle before Yule Eve or to blow out its flame instead of using a snuffer. Saving a piece of the Yule candle is said to bring a person good luck throughout the coming year.

A Druid priest. (An illustration from William Stukeley's Stonehenge, *first published in 1740)*

Yuletide Spellcraft

Yule Pudding Spell

A Yule wishing spell from Victorian times is as follows: If you have a wish that you would like to come true, concentrate upon it as you stir the Yule pudding three times around in a clockwise direction. If your wish involves prosperity, place a thimble into the mixture before stirring it. If your wish is of an amatory nature, a ring is the appropriate charm to add. Be sure to keep your wish a secret and, most importantly, be careful what you wish for because you will likely obtain it!

Mistletoe Spell for Luck

With a consecrated ritual dagger, ceremonially cut a piece of mistletoe at sunrise on the Winter Solstice. As you do this, recite the following magickal incantation three times:

> *Golden bough and witch's broom,*
> *Thy sacred names are spoken.*
> *By dagger's blade I conjure thee*
> *To see all bad luck broken.*
> *Harming none, this spell is done.*
> *So mote it be!*

Hang the white-berried plant over the front door of your house and good luck will be brought to all who dwell within.

Mistletoe, which is also known by the folk names "golden bough" and "witch's broom," is also said to possess the power to heal wounds and protect against evil, fire, illness, and spells of sorcery. The ancient priests and priestesses of Druidism revered the mistletoe as a highly magickal charm.

Yule Candle Spell

For good luck to smile upon you throughout the coming year, perform the following spell at midnight on the Winter Solstice: Anoint a Yule candle with three drops of frankincense and myrrh oil while projecting your positive thoughts and emotions into it. With the blade of a consecrated athame, trace the symbol of the pentagram three times in the air above the candle. Light its wick with a match, and then recite the following incantation nine times:

> *Candle of Yule, with flame so bright,*
> *You shall burn throughout this night.*
> *Conjure good luck to be here,*
> *All throughout the coming year.*
> *So mote it be!*

Allow the Yule candle to burn, undisturbed, until sunrise. (A safe place to keep a burning Yule candle overnight is either in the bathtub or kitchen sink.) When the time comes to put out the candle, extinguish the flame with a candle snuffer or by pinching it out between your moistened fingertips. Take care not to scatter your good luck to the wind by blowing it out!

Yule Cake Spell for Good Luck

For good luck to be by your side throughout the coming year, bake a Yule cake. (In England, Yule cakes were traditionally sliced, toasted, and soaked in spicy ale.) On the day of the old festival of the Sun's rebirth (December 25) cut a portion of the cake and set it aside until New Year's Day. Keeping it in the freezer is recommended. Eat the slice of Yule cake on the first day of January to ensure that bad luck is kept at bay.

Here's a recipe for old-fashioned Yule cake:

In a large bowl, sift together 3/4 cup flour, 3/4 cup sugar, 1/2 teaspoon baking powder, 1/2 teaspoon salt, 1/3 teaspoon cinnamon, 1/3 teaspoon allspice, and 1/3 teaspoon mace. Add 1 1/2 cups Brazil nuts (shelled), 1 1/2 cups walnut halves, 1 cup pitted dates, 1/2 cup red maraschino cherries (well-drained), and 1/2 cup dried currants and seedless raisins mixed together and soaked overnight in brandy or whiskey. Mix well. In a separate bowl, beat together until fluffy three eggs and 1 tablespoon of either vanilla or almond extract. Pour the egg mixture over the fruits and nuts and mix well. Pour the cake batter into a well-greased loaf pan that has been lined on the bottom and sides with a double thickness of greased baking parchment. (The baking parchment prevents the cake from drying out and scorching.) Bake in a preheated 300-degree oven for 1 hour and 45 minutes (or until the cake is firm on top). Remove cake from oven and allow it to cool before removing from pan. Discard the baking parchment. Sprinkle the cake generously with the spirit of your choice. Wrap it well in aluminum foil, put it in a sealed tin, and then store it in a cool place.

Spell to Banish Bad Luck

If your life is plagued by many problems and you feel that you have been jinxed with bad luck, this simple spell from olden times may be able to help you out. On Yule morning, before anyone else in the household wakes and gets out of bed, take a broom, open the front door, and symbolically sweep all trouble and bad luck from the threshold. As you do this, repeat the following incantation:

Sweep, sweep, be gone all woe,
From the threshold now you go!
Sweep, sweep, I shall not weep,
Bad luck flee and good luck keep!

Mistletoe Love Spell

To win a man's heart you must pluck a leaf from the mistletoe under which two lovers have kissed on Yule. If a kiss under the mistletoe has been shared between yourself and the man whose heart you wish to bind to you, this is all the better for the spell! During a day and hour ruled by Venus, and when the Moon is waxing or full, secretly prick the man's initials on the leaf with a new sewing needle that has been dipped in rose oil. As you do this, focus all of your thoughts upon the object of your desires and visualize him as already yours. State aloud your intent and then thrice repeat the following incantation:

Plant of magick,
Leaf of green,
Let him whose initials are pricked on thee
Grow in his heart a desire for me.
Empower this spell,
Bewitch him well
With love's enchanting charm and glamour,
Until for me he is enamored.
By the power of Venus,
So mote it be!

Using the same needle and a length of pink thread, stitch the leaf to the inside of your brassiere so that it rests near your heart. As long as it remains there, the man whose affections you desire shall be bound to you.

Mistletoe Love Divinations

To conjure a dream in which the face or name of your future husband is revealed unto you, you will need a sprig of mistletoe taken from a churchyard. On the eve of Yule, place the sprig beneath your pillow and pray to Morpheus (the god of dreams) to send you a prophetic dream. Lay your head upon the pillow, close your eyes, and allow yourself to drift off to sleep. If no face or name appears to you while you dream, this is an indication that you shall not wed within the coming 12 months. Do not repeat the divination until the next Yule Eve.

Another way in which the Yuletide mistletoe is traditionally used for love divination is as follows: To discover whether your future husband will have an agreeable or disagreeable disposition, take a piece of mistletoe under which two lovers have shared a kiss, wrap it in a silk or satin handkerchief, and then store it away for 12 months until the next Yule.

At the witching hour that marks the beginning of the Winter Solstice, unwrap the year-old piece of mistletoe and cast it into a fire. As it burns, you must carefully observe the flames. If they are steady, this is a good sign that your future husband will be agreeable in his disposition. However, if they sputter, this indicates a husband who will possess a bad temper.

Chapter 12

Sybil Leek

O ne of the most popular spellcasters of the 20th century, and perhaps the woman most instrumental in spreading Witchcraft in America, was Sybil Leek. Her classic *Diary of a Witch* was the first book on contemporary Witchcraft that I ever read. Her words spoke to my soul, and from that day forward I knew in my mind and in my heart that the Old Religion was the right path for me to follow. I have long held a deep respect and admiration for Sybil Leek, and I owe her much gratitude, which is one of the reasons I have chosen to devote this chapter to her. Had it not been for her positive influence upon me at the age of 10, a rewarding role as a public spokesperson for the Craft and a successful career as an author of Witchcraft books might not have been in my future. Another reason for this chapter is that the fascinating story of Sybil Leek's life journey is a vital part of Craft history, and one that I am confident will inspire and enlighten many of the aspiring Witches and spellcrafters who read it.

Born in Midlands, England on February 22, 1923 (or 1917, depending upon the source) Leek was said to have come from a long line of Hereditary Witches. (Molly Leigh, a famous 17th-century Witch, was one of her ancestors.) She said that all of her relatives were gifted with clairvoyant powers and that her family's involvement in the Old Religion could be traced back to the year 1134. In one of her books it is mentioned that her family "was at home with all sorts of occult happenings."

At the age of 9, Sybil first met occultist and ceremonial magician Aleister Crowley. A close friend of the family, he inspired her to write poetry and taught her the importance of words of power and the power of sound. It is said that he once told her grandmother that he believed Sybil would someday follow in his footsteps.

Sybil began writing at the age of 15, and by the time she was 16 she had her own radio program. Shortly after turning 16, she married a famous pianist-conductor and accompanied him in his travels throughout Europe. Although they were very much in love, the marriage was ill fated, and two years after her wedding day Leek became a young widow.

It was in southern France that Leek was initiated into the Craft and appointed High Priestess of a coven, taking the place of an elderly aunt who recently died. She returned to England and found a home among the Gypsies in the heart of the New Forest. She became a member of a 700-year old coven, and in time took on the role of its high priestess. She married her second husband and gave birth to two sons, Stephen and Julian, who were said to have inherited their mother's clairvoyant abilities. She also ran three antique shops, that proved to be successful business endeavors.

A mystical experience changed Sybil Leek's life in the early 1950s. One day while strolling through the New Forest, her personal revelation began with the sight of a solitary witch hazel tree in bloom. From its broken boughs, according to Leek, "a bright blue light grew until it surrounded the whole tree...I stood still and heard voices telling me the path I must take in my life. As I listened, the light from the tree began to spread out toward me until I too was enveloped in it. A great sense of peacefulness came over me, impossible to describe in words, but through the light I felt like a newborn baby still attached to its mother, ready for someone to cut the umbilical cord and give it an individual life of its own. At that moment, the shining silver-blue light divided, one half still surrounding the witch hazel tree and the other enfolding me." After the light faded, it was clear to Leek that her purpose in this life was to be an evangelist for the Old Religion.

After the Witchcraft Act was repealed in England in 1951 and Witchcraft was no longer on the books as a crime, Leek bravely came out of the proverbial "broom closet." She publicly announced herself a Witch and soon found herself standing in the center of the media spotlight. Tourists, autograph seekers, and the media descended upon the New Forest. Public knowledge of Leek's involvement with the Craft resulted in the decline of business at her antique shop. In addition, Leek's public disclosure of her spiritual beliefs and magickal practices prompted her landlord to refuse renewing her lease unless a public denouncement of the Old Religion was made. Proud of her Pagan heritage and one step away from worldwide acclaim, Leek refused.

The 1960s proved to be a transitional decade for Leek. She closed up her shop in the New Forest and left England to pursue her fame and fortune on the other side of the Atlantic. After her decision to make the United States her new home, Leek moved to New York City and then relocated to Los Angeles, where she met Israel Regardie, an occultist and one-time secretary of Aleister Crowley.

Astrology, the "science of the stars," interested Leek, and she pursued it on a professional level, eventually publishing and editing her own astrological journal.

Diary of a Witch, Sybil Leek's first book, was published in 1968. Revealing to the world the beliefs and practices of a modern Witch, the book became a best seller for Leek and she embarked on the media tour circuit with a goal to dispel the myths and negative stereotypes about those who followed the Old Religion. Her efforts, however, were not always successful.

After accepting an invitation to appear as a guest on the *Today* show and expecting to engage in a serious discussion about Witchcraft as a valid religion, Leek discovered that the NBC programmers had something else in mind. They expected her to entertain viewers by stirring a bubbling cauldron, reciting a Shakespearean "double, double, toil and trouble" incantation, and cackling. She refused to take part in the stereotyping and theatrics, and instead used her appearance on the show to educate the public about the Craft.

One of the most popular spellcasters of the 20th century, and perhaps the woman most instrumental in spreading Witchcraft in America, was Sybil Leek. (United Press International)

Sybil Leek's definition of a Witch was "a woman who has unusual powers of good and evil. These powers bear a direct relationship to one's understanding of religious truths. How these powers that come from a higher force are to be used depends entirely upon the intentions of the person."

In magickal practice, Sybil Leek's specialty was Celtic Witchcraft, but through her prolific writing she shared her vast knowledge of various magickal traditions, including Voodoo, sorcery, and candle magick. The key to a spellcaster's success, according to Dame Leek, "is the way he synchronizes his words, the material ingredients, the cause, and his own emotions so that all are in harmony with a specific time." Simply casting a spell during the proper lunar phase is not enough, for "within each day there are also especially appropriate hours." In addition, Leek cited "ignorance of the fact that spells must be performed according to a strict ritual with necessary preparations made well in advance" as the number-one cause of spellcasting failure.

One of Sybil Leek's successful methods of candle magick is to simultaneously burn two candles, one corresponding to your astrological sign, and the other corresponding to your purpose. (See Chapter 6 for complete lists of astrological and magickal candle colors.) According to Leek, ordinary household candles should not be employed for candle magick. Candles of the appropriate color should be purchased and kept wrapped up and out of view until used. Whether used in spells for good or evil, candles should always be anointed with the appropriate essential oil before being lit. Prepare an incantation in advance (one that precisely states your intent), memorize it, and then destroy the paper upon which you wrote it.

Setting her apart from many other Witches of her time, Sybil Leek disapproved of ritual nudity but believed that cursing was justified against one's enemies. However, in her book, *Sybil Leek's Book of Curses,* she warns that "swearwords, curses, and hexes add up to nothing good for mankind." She also believed in "witch's marks" and said that she and other women in her family line possessed them.

Introduced to the divinatory art of scrying (crystal gazing) during her childhood in England, Sybil Leek felt that of all present day fortunetellers the crystal gazer was the person most likely to possess true psychic talents. However, she was "suspicious of modern so-called crystal balls as divining objects." She believed that pure rock crystal was the "true instrument of scrying," and any object manufactured from synthetic materials was incapable of offering a scryer successful results. Fortune-telling interested Leek so much that she wrote a book on the subject, published in 1969.

Sybil Leek also wrote and spoke a great deal about the subject of life after death. Her belief in reincarnation was reinforced by a strange experience she encountered while giving a lecture on psychic phenomena before an audience of the Theosophical Society in St. Louis. According to Leek in her book *Reincarnation: The Second Chance,* while gazing out into the crowd, "the shining light I had first seen in the New Forest seemed to rise like a flame from the center of the hall and move toward me. Within the light I could distinguish the face of an elderly woman, a face I did not recognize. She and the light invaded the platform, surrounding me, and somehow I felt that the woman had merged into my own body. It was not a frightening experience at all. I felt exhilarated, as I always do when the shining light bathes me, and I started to talk to the audience with complete confidence. I spoke only about reincarnation—without any awareness of what I was saying. When the hectic question-and-answer period that followed was over, crowds of people mounted the platform. I felt released from the light; I had regained my identity."

Leek later realized that the woman who had appeared in her vision and guided her was Madame Helena Blavanskyma, cofounder of the Theosophical Society and a woman to whom Leek bore a striking resemblance.

Psychic powers were one of Sybil Leek's greatest talents and she frequently taught classes on ESP development. She could clearly see certain events before they happened as though she was actually living through them. At times the future would be prophesied to her by a distant voice. She did not consider her sixth sense to be a special gift. Rather, it was simply another form of energy to her, like electricity, and a skill that she believed could be taught to anyone, as long as the student was willing to put in the effort required to learn it. Ten generations of her family were said to have possessed extrasensory perception and she was convinced that it was her family's Celtic heritage that facilitated this ability.

Sybil Leek was said to have had an IQ of 164. She wrote more than 60 books and had an internationally syndicated column. She is also remembered for her prediction of the Kennedy assassinations and the election of Richard Nixon to the presidency. (On the misfortunes experienced by the Kennedy family,

Leek said, "The reincarnationalist is likely to assume that the roots of their tragedies lie in past incarnations, and that future incarnations will bring a better lot in life for those Kennedys who—as they all will—come back.")

In addition to writing and lecturing, Sybil Leek devoted a portion of her time to visiting places reputed to be the sites of paranormal activity. Along with her friend and associate, Professor Hans Holzer, she investigated San Diego's infamous Whaley House, said to be the "most haunted house in America." She psychically picked up that the spirit of the man after whom the house was named was angry that another house (the Derby-Pendleton House) had been placed upon the Whaley property. And although his enemies and rivals were long gone, he still felt a need to guard his house, which explained why his restless spirit continued to roam the historic property. While in trance at the Whaley House, Leek unexpectedly became a medium for the centuries-old spirit of a Russian man who had died in the San Diego area while on an expedition to hunt sea otters.

Leek was quite fond of birds and snakes. Her animal familiars were a jackdaw (a relative of the raven) named Mr. Hotfoot Jackson, and a pair of pet boa constrictors. Mr. Hotfoot Jackson was said to have accompanied Leek to all of her coven meetings and excursions to investigate haunted houses. She described him as "an exceptional bird" whose "awareness of any psychic phenomenon was amazing."

The last years of Leek's life were spent battling illness. Five days before Halloween in 1982 she passed away in Melbourne, Florida. Described as "a Renaissance woman" and "a free spirit," she never lost her sense of wonder, and departed this world holding firmly onto her personal belief that good always conquers evil.

A wise woman, a crusader for Witches everywhere, a prolific author, and a colorful personality, Sybil Leek will always hold a revered place in Craft history. She is missed by many, but as long as her memory and published works continue to inspire and enlighten us, her spirit shall never fade away.

Thank you, Sybil. And blessed be.

Chapter 13

Black Magick

Magick in itself is neither good nor evil, neither white nor black. It is a neutral energy force that does not think, feel, love, hate, or know right from wrong. Its positive or negative current (much like that of a battery) is determined by the will and intent of the practitioner.

When negative magickal energy in any form (such as curses, hexes, psychic attacks, Voodoo dolls, evil wishes, and so on) is employed with the intent to bring harm to others in one way of another, it is classified as black magick.

It is extremely naive to believe that the Wiccan Rede or the karmic Law of Three prevents black magick from being practiced. Although most contemporary Witches (especially those of the Wiccan traditions) are opposed to the use of black magick and strictly adhere to the Rede of "harm none," there are others who are not in alignment with, or intimidated by, the Wiccan's Rede and Threefold Law and who would not hesitate to summon forth dark destructive powers, proclaim curses, and deliver hexes to enemies or rivals if they felt an inclination to do so. Voodoo, sorcery, hoodoo folk magick, hexcraft, and Satanic Witchcraft are but several examples of magickally oriented religions and practices that routinely employ black magick, in addition to white, and sometimes gray, magick.

Whether such practitioners are unaware, unbelieving, or unconcerned that their every action (both bad and good) brings forth upon themselves an inevitable corresponding reaction has no bearing on the fact that black magick has always been, and most likely will always be, practiced throughout the world. And the sad and frightening truth is that any targeted individual, regardless of his or her race, culture, religious or non-religious beliefs, or level of education, can easily become a victim of someone's spell.

This chapter will not instruct you on how to use black magick to curse others. It will not help you to master the art of afflicting psychic attacks, reveal the dark secrets of the evil eye, show you how to evoke demonic entities to do your bidding, or teach you how to use spellcraft to get even with those against whom you seek revenge. Instead, it will instruct you on how to keep yourself, your loved ones, and your home safely protected against the negative effects of black magick. It will also teach you how to recognize evil, how to distinguish true curses and hexes from mere unlucky coincidences, and what to do if you believe that you have fallen victim to someone's evil intent.

The first, and perhaps most important, step is to be aware that black magick is quite real and it works. It is foolish to deny its existence and naive to believe that any guardian spirit, angel, or god or goddess of your choice will always watch over you and keep you safe from all harm. This is akin to believing that a loaded gun cannot possibly harm you because you have convinced yourself that the gun does not exist and therefore has no power over you. You are only fooling yourself. And as far as faith in otherworldly beings is concerned, it is a sobering fact that many religious faithful are injured or killed by guns every day without divine intervention of any kind stepping in to save them.

The frontispiece to Magica de spectris et apparition-ibus spiritu, *published in the year 1656.*

Curses and Hexes

Many people use the words "curse" and "hex" in an interchangeable fashion to mean a spell that is intended to bring harm or death to a victim. In the Pennsylvania Dutch tradition of Witchcraft, a hex can be a spell generated by either black or white magick. (The word "hex" derives from the German "hexen," which means "Witch.") Additionally, some contemporary Witches call their binding spells hexes.

Although there are many modern Witches who regard the laying of curses to be unethical and a violation of the Wiccan Rede, there are others, such as the brujas of Mexico, the stregas of Italy, and the brauchers of the Pennsylvania Dutch, who believe that cursing is justified against one's enemies.

Can Curses Kill?

The answer is yes, and the critical factor in death by black magick (or hex death, as it is sometimes called) is belief. If an individual believes strongly enough that a curse laid upon him will end his life, the curse will probably succeed in doing just that.

The mind is a remarkably powerful instrument, and the concept of mind over matter should not be taken lightly. Consider this: If the mind can be used to heal, it can also be used to kill!

In *The Encyclopedia of Witches and Witchcraft*, author Rosemary Ellen Guiley states, "Hex death is largely a self-fulfilling prophecy." She goes on to say that "if the victim believes his cursed situation to be hopeless, he begins to experience feelings of helplessness, incompetence, despair, and worthlessness. Illness sets in, which the victim has no desire to fight, and eventually he succumbs."

> *"This is the curse of every evil deed*
> *That, propagating still, it brings forth evil."*
> —Southey

I receive a number of letters each year from individuals around the world and from all walks of life who, for one reason or another, are convinced that they are a victim of black magick. Their fears and feelings of desperation are quite sincere, and they seek my help in bringing an end to the curses, hexes, jinxes, and whammies that they believe are adversely affecting their lives. However, in nearly all cases, the manifestations of black magick and sorcery are nothing more than a passing streak of bad luck, overactive imaginations (sometimes coupled with paranoia), and, in some instances, the effects of one's own bad karma.

Luckily, bad luck streaks are temporary, although in some cases they are self-inflicted through negative thoughts and feelings and self-destructive inclinations. Overactive imaginations can often be put to rest by meditation, positive thinking exercises, and so forth, and paranoia by psychiatric counseling and medication. Karma, on the other hand, is a more serious matter and one even more difficult to treat, but doing good for others is definitely a step in the right direction in the restoration of karmic balance.

At this point you may be wondering to yourself what the symptoms of a magickal attack are and how to distinguish those that are the result of black magick from those that are not.

The symptoms of a magickal attack, according to Paul Huson in his book *Mastering Witchcraft,* "can range from recurrent nightmares, through runs of unbelievably bad luck, psychosomatic disturbances and allergies, often accompanied by poltergeist manifestations, to outright cases of lunacy or even sudden death."

With the exception of the poltergeist activity, the aforementioned list of symptoms generally have a non-occult basis, and before drawing any definite conclusions about magickal attacks, it is advisable to obtain the opinion of a qualified physician or mental health specialist.

Recurring nightmares, often marked by occult or Satanic symbolism, are the most common telltale sign that black magick is at work. One easy way to determine whether or not your nigthmares are magickally induced is to keep a watchful eye on the moon and its phases. Nightmares of this nature almost always reach their peak at the time of the new moon, rather than when it is full. The same holds true for magickally induced illnesses and bouts of bad luck.

In most cases, when a curse or a hex has been directed against you, there will be a general sense of evil in the air. The stronger the black magick, the more negatively charged the atmosphere around you becomes. And, naturally, the more psychically sensitive you are, the greater your perception of the evil vibrations will be.

A second method of discovering if evil spells are afoot is to consult a deck of Tarot cards, the *I Ching* (Book of Changes), rune stones, a crystal ball, a pendulum, or some other tool of divination. This method is commonly employed by Witches, psychics, and other individuals who are skilled in the divinatory arts.

Another way to tell if you are the victim of a magickal attack is to ask yourself the following questions:

1. Has anyone, at any time, hinted at or openly pro-claimed a curse against you? (Many practitioners of the Black Arts make it a point to inform their victims in one way or another that a curse has been laid upon them in order to add potency to their black magick. This is called "planting the seed," and it lays the groundwork for a magickal attack. In many instances, when a person is aware that a curse has been placed upon him and is led to believe (even if only on a sub-conscious level) that his fate is sealed, he will eventu-ally bring about his own demise.

2. Do you have any enemies or rivals? (These can include the people you work with, schoolmates, neigh-bors, ex-lovers, and so on.)

3. Are you acquainted with anyone who is involved in, or has demonstrated any sort of interest in, the occult or the magickal arts? If so, have you done anything to cross this person?

4. Do you know of anyone who is jealous of you or would have any reason to seek revenge against you? (Hatred, jealousy, revenge, and, in some cases, lust are the general factors that motivate a magickal attack.)

5. Before your misfortunes began, did you encounter anyone who had strange, mesmerizing eyes or from whom you picked up "weird vibes" for no apparent reason? Certain individuals—regardless of gender, race, or nationality—are born with a strange and de-structive supernatural power known as the evil eye. One venomous glance, known as an "overlooking," from such an individual is said to result in bad luck, illness, injury, poverty, loss of love, madness, and even death for the victim. Although the evil eye can be cast voluntarily, usually motivated by envy or revenge, it is believed that most of the time it happens involuntarily, with the over-looker being completely unaware that he or she is casting it.

6. Have you been experiencing any unexplained sharp jabbing pains in the fashion of a pin or sharp nail being stuck into a Voodoo doll?

7. Are you suffering from any physical symptoms for which your doctor has been unable to find a cause?

8. Do your symptoms always begin sometime after the sun has set and disappear before the sun rises the following morning? Magickal attacks almost always take place at night, often at the witching hour or during a planetary hour of Mars or Saturn. Many cursers like to do their dirty work during the wee hours of the morning, when their potential victims are fast asleep, for this is generally the time when most people's psychic defenses are down and they are most vulnerable to a magickal attack.

9. Has anybody recently made any strange body gestures (particularly hand gestures) in your direction? Some sorcerers deliver their curses by a method known as the "hand-of-power gesture." This involves outstretching the left arm with fist clenched and the index and middle fingers pointing straight at the victim. Sometimes this is carried out while standing only on the right foot and with the right eye closed, which is an ancient method of projecting magickal power and is associated with the Druids. Some sorcerers can also deliver a curse simply by pointing an index finger at their victim, while others use a gesture known as the "devil's horns" (middle and fourth fingers pinned down with the thumb; index and little fingers extended). Interestingly, the sign of the "devil's horns" is also used as a defense against the evil eye, especially in Italy and the Balkan states.

If your answer to any of these questions is "yes," there is a good possibility that some form of black magick is being used against you!

What to Do

Once you have determined that you are on the receiving end of any kind of magickal attack, it is important for you to remain calm (fear helps curses to take effect), stay focused, and immediately plan your defense strategy. The best weapon against black magick is countermagick, which consists of protective anti-sorcery amulets, candle rituals, herbs and oils that help to remove curses and evil from your life, various psychic defense methods, bindings to render a sorcerer or sorceress powerless, spells to create a protective shield against attacks of black magick, spells to break hexes and curses, and spells that redirect the malevolent energy of a curse back to its sender.

> *The doing evil to avoid an evil cannot be good.*
> —Coleridge

It is a perfectly natural human response to feel anger, hatred, a desire for vengeance, and other negative emotions at the thought of being magickally victimized by another. Some individuals, in the tradition of "an eye for an eye," feel that one good curse deserves another. However, speaking from experience, this rarely accomplishes anything except for putting a vicious circle of black magick into motion, not to mention the karmic implications and the risk of your curse backfiring should your bolt of magickal power miss its target.

The age-old art of magickal warfare should, under no circumstances, be undertaken lightly, especially by the novice Witch or spellcaster. Heed well my words, or prepare to learn thy lessons the hard way!

Whenever the fires of an all out "Witch war" are kindled, the opposing sides may engage in a magickal duel until the one with the stronger power prevails. Such battles can rage on for months or years, and in some cases carry over into future lifetimes.

In *Mastering Witchcraft,* Paul Huson states, "In matters of occult warfare, passive defense is the most effective type of retaliation." This is indeed an important rule of the Craft, and should never be forgotten or ignored. Being adequately protected against a magickal attack will ensure that any and all curses delivered unto you will rebound upon the curser, with the effects felt threefold.

The Purple Candle Spell

In addition to banishing illness, purple candles are traditionally used by Witches to reverse curses and cast them back on their senders. According to Sybil Leek in *Sybil Leek's Book of Curses,* "Purple candles are powerful against black magick practitioners who are not very concerned with doing good to anyone."

When the moon is on the wane, inscribe the name of your curser upon a new purple candle, as well as upon a piece of parchment. Place the parchment beneath the candle, and then anoint the candle with three drops of uncrossing oil, rosemary oil, or van-van oil. Light the candle with a match (do not use a cigarette lighter), and thrice repeat the following incantation:

> *By the power of the four Elements,*
> *By the power of the ancient gods,*
> *Be thou [name of curser] stopped!*
> *Let the curse return to whence it cometh*
> *And threefold let it be unto thee!*
> *As I will it, so mote it be.*

Allow the candle to burn itself out and then bury the remaining wax in the earth and trace the sign of the Banishing Pentagram in the air above it using the blade of your consecrated athame. (To draw a Banishing Pentagram, begin at the lower left point of the star and move up in a clockwise fashion to the top point, down to the lower right point, up to the upper left point, straight across to the upper right point, and finally, down to the lower left point.)

If you wish to simply break the curse and remove the curser from your path without bringing to him or her any physical harm, perform the above spell using a black candle instead of a purple one, and change the incantation to the following:

> *By the power of the four elements,*
> *By the power of the ancient gods,*
> *Be thou [name of curser] stopped!*
> *From my path may this enemy be removed*
> *And may I be released forthwith*
> *From his (her) evil intent!*
> *Harming none, this spell is done.*
> *By law of three, so mote it be.*

Poppet Spell

To break a curse, stuff a cloth poppet with nettles at the witching hour on a Tuesday or Saturday when the moon is waning. If you know the name of the person who has cursed you, write it upon the poppet using dragon's blood ink. And if you are fortunate enough to have a photograph of your curser, cut his or her face out of the picture with a pair of scissors and then glue it to the poppet's face.

The next step is to take the poppet in your hands, blow your breath upon it to "activate" it, and then say:

> *You are he (she) who curses me.*
> *I banish you! So mote it be.*

The final step is to bury the poppet in the earth or to set it on fire using the flame of a purple candle and then bury the ashes. Take your consecrated athame in your power hand and with the tip of the blade trace three Banishing Pentagrams in the air above the poppet's "grave."

A Mirror Spell to Bind a Sorcerer's Powers

To perform this highly effective spell you will need a small mirror, a photograph or drawing of the person who has used his evil powers of sorcery against you, a piece of black velvet large enough to be completely wrapped around the mirror, and a length of black cord.

When the moon is on the wane and the planetary hour corresponds to Saturn, light a black candle that has been anointed by any occult oil designed for breaking curses. Take the photograph or drawing and lay it flat over the mirror with its image side facing the mirror's reflective surface. If you so desire, you may use a bit of tape to keep the photograph or drawing in place. Cover the mirror with the black velvet and then take the cord and tie it around the mirror, criss-crossing it to form an "X" design. Holding the mirror in your hands, concentrate upon binding your adversary and nine times "breathe" the following incantation over the mirror:

> *By mirror, by velvet, by cord of black,*
> *I bind thee well from all attack.*
> *From thine own spells be unprotected*
> *When back to thee they are reflected.*
> *Harm only thyself by evil times three,*
> *For as I will it, so mote it be!*

The final step of the binding spell is to dig a hole in the earth and, without uttering a word and without allowing the eyes of any other to be upon you, place the velvet-covered mirror inside the hole and then fill it in with the dug-up dirt. Take your consecrated athame in your power hand and with its blade trace the symbol of a Banishing Pentagram in the air above the spot where the mirror has been buried. The spell is now complete.

An Image Candle Binding Spell

To bind the evil powers of a sorcerer or sorceress, you will need a black human image candle of the appropriate gender to represent your adversary, a length of black cord, and any occult oils used for bindings, such as rosemary oil or Turn Back Oil.

Perform this binding spell when the moon is in a waning phase and when the planetary hour corresponds to Saturn, which is the ideal time for performing bindings.

Begin by inscribing the name of your adversary (if known) upon the candle. If you know only that you have been cursed but do not know who has inflicted it upon you, then simply inscribe upon the candle, "The One Who Sends Me Curses." Anoint the candle with three drops of the oil, and then repeat the following incantation:

> *No longer is this candle*
> *Merely wax and wick.*
> *By the power of the ancient gods,*
> *By the power of the ancient goddesses,*
> *And by the power of my will is it now*
> *The evil one who has cursed me.*

Take the black cord and tightly wrap it nine times around the candle. Knot it and then thrice repeat:

> *Evil one, evil one*
> *Thy spell is now undone!*
> *No more harm shall come from thee,*
> *Hold now the power to curse none!*
> *This is my will, so mote it be.*

Wrap the image candle in a piece of black velvet or black satin, and then either bury it in the earth or hide it in a secret place where it will remain undisturbed indefinitely.

Magickal Oils

There are a number of magickal occult oils that possess the power to break curses and keep an individual safe against future magickal attacks.

Rose geranium oil and rosemary oil are ideal for magickal baths to remove curses, hexes, and all evil influences from your life. Add nine drops of either oil to your warm bath water when the moon is waning, and bathe by the light of three burning candles, one purple (to break curses), one red (for protection), and one white (to restore balance and for positive and powerful vibrations).

Both rose geranium and rosemary oils can also be used as chakra anointing oils to debilitate any curses directed against you. Anoint each of your seven chakras once daily for seven days in a row.

Add nine drops of Uncrossing Oil to one ounce of rosemary oil, or seven drops of van-van oil to one ounce of Uncrossing Oil to create a powerful anti-hex formula. To release your home from any curses, sprinkle any of the above-mentioned oil mixtures, or angelica oil, in a circle around your house, beginning at the East side of the property and working in a clockwise fashion as you chant the following incantation:

> *As this magick spell is spoken,*
> *Curses near and far be broken!*

For maximum effectiveness, repeat the spell for nine nights in a row, beginning on the first night of the waning moon.

When worn daily on the body, African Ju-Ju Oil, one of the most powerful of African oils, is said to keep a person untouchable by any curse or hex. Bergamot, a popular oil among many Voodoo practitioners, is also reputed to offer protection against curses when rubbed into the palms of the hands.

In addition to the aforementioned occult oils, the following essential oils and blends, available at most Occult shops, are used by practitioners from various magickal traditions to protect against, to break, and to return curses, hexes, evil wishes, jinxes, and negative energy:

- ⊛ Chili pepper oil.
- ⊛ Clearance Oil.
- ⊛ Cyclamen oil.
- ⊛ Dragon's Blood Oil.
- ⊛ Fiery Wall of Protection.
- ⊛ Flying Devil Oil.

- ✸ Geranium oil.
- ✸ Guinea Oil.
- ✸ Hex-Breaking Oil.
- ✸ Holly oil.
- ✸ Jasper Oil.
- ✸ Jinx Removing Oil.
- ✸ Ju-Ju Oil.
- ✸ Juniper oil.
- ✸ Justo Juez Oil.
- ✸ Mars Oil.
- ✸ Melissa Oil.
- ✸ Mimosa oil.
- ✸ Protection Oil.
- ✸ Reverse Evil Oil.
- ✸ Reversible Oil.
- ✸ Sassafras oil.
- ✸ Saturn Oil.
- ✸ Scotch pine oil.
- ✸ Solomon's Seal Oil.
- ✸ Spell Breaker/Breaking Oil.
- ✸ Verbena oil.
- ✸ Vetivert oil.
- ✸ Wintergreen oil.
- ✸ Witchbane Oil.
- ✸ Wolf's Eye Oil.
- ✸ Wormwood oil.

Cat's Eye Amulet

The cat's eye is a stone possessing great amuletic power to ward off all curses and negativity and to deflect them back to their senders.

For maximum effectiveness against any type of magickal or psychic attack, wear a cat's eye in the form of a ring or a pendant, and remember to anoint it daily with a drop of Cat's Eye Oil. If you are unable to find Cat's Eye Oil in your local occult shop, you may use any of the aforementioned oils to anoint your amulet.

If a curse laid against you is a particularly powerful one, it may be beneficial to employ more than one cat's eye stone. Wear them at all times, even while bathing and sleeping. Take care not to remove them until you are absolutely certain that all threats of evil have passed.

A Hex-breaking Candle Ritual

Perform this candle-burning ritual during a planetary hour of Saturn when the moon is in a waning phase. If the moon should also be in the astrological sign of Aries or Scorpio, this is all the better!

Begin the ritual by invoking the four Elements of Air, Fire, Water, and Earth, casting a circle in a clockwise fashion, and then lighting incense, altar candles, and astral candle. (See Chapter 6 for additional information on candle-burning ritual procedures.)

On the center of the altar, place a purple, seven-knob candle that has been anointed with any occult oil designed for hex-breaking. Light the candle with a match, and thrice recite either of the following incantations:

> *By the powers of wick and wax*
> *Let this hex now be reversed!*
> *Remove all evil from my path*
> *And let its sender be now cursed!*
> *So mote it be.*

Or:

> *Hexes now be broken,*
> *Evil be turned back,*
> *By the power of white magick,*
> *Triumphant over black!*
> *So mote it be.*

Allow one knob of the candle to melt away and then extinguish the candle by smothering the flame with a candle snuffer or by pinching it out with the moistened tips of your thumb and index finger. Release the Elements by offering thanks and bidding farewell to them, and uncast the circle in a counter-clockwise fashion.

Repeat the ritual for the next six nights in a row, burning one knob of the candle during each ritual. After the close of the candle-burning ritual on the final night, take whatever wax is left over from the candle, wrap it in a piece of purple linen, and then bury it in the earth. Take your consecrated athame in your power hand and, with the tip of its blade, trace the powerful sign of the Banishing Pentagram in the air above the spot. The hex-breaking candle ritual is now complete. Repeat it at the next waning moon if necessary.

17th-century Countermagick

In 17th-century New England, one of the most popular and reputedly effective methods of dealing with curse and turning the evil back upon the instigator was to fill a cast iron pot with the urine of the bewitched victim. Over a fire the pot would be placed until the urine came to a boil, at which point a number of pins or needles would be added. This was done in the belief that the pins or needles brought great torment to the woman or man who inflicted the curse. When the urine was completely boiled away, the curse was broken and the victim released from the Witch's power.

In the Massachusetts seaport of Salem, where the infamous Witch trials and hangings of 1692 took place, spellbreaking cakes made from rye meal mixed with the urine of the bewitched victim were baked in ovens and then fed to the animal thought to be the Witch's imp or familiar. It was believed that when the animal consumed the cake, whatever evil spell or spells that had been cast over the victim would be immediately lifted.

*An old woodcut depicting sorceresses casting spells with the aid of
demons and animal familiars. (The Fortean Picture Library)*

A Witch Bottle to Protect Against Magickal Attacks

For protection against magickal attacks by those who seek
to harm, harass, or destroy you, conjure the magick of a Witch
Bottle when the moon is waning and the planetary hour corresponds to Saturn.

Take a small glass bottle and fill it to the brim with the following items: black pebbles, nails, a bit of fur clipped from the
tail of an all-black cat, black bird feathers, berries and/or the bark
of the rowan tree (also known as witchbane), and a High John
the Conqueror root (poisonous).

Seal the bottle tightly with a cork or lid and then carefully
pour melted wax from a purple candle over the seal. Holding the
bottle in your hands, concentrate upon your intent and thrice
recite the following incantation:

> *By waning moon and Saturn's hour*
> *Witch's bottle I empower*
> *Thee with magick strong and true*
> *To every wicked spell undo,*
> *And worketh for me as a charm*
> *To keep me day and night from harm.*
> *I conjure thee by law of three, this is my will,*
> *So mote it be!*

Take your consecrated athame in your power hand and touch the top of the Witch Bottle with the tip of its blade as you bless it in the names of the Goddess and Her consort, the Horned God. Seal the spell by burning a pinch of sandalwood incense over a hot charcoal block in an incense burner.

Bury the Witch Bottle in a hole dug at the farthest corner of your property, or hide it in a kitchen cupboard or some other place in your home where it will be out of view and undisturbed.

To Unhex a House

At the witching hour of Saint John's Eve (June 22), burn 13 yarrow sticks in the fireplace. (If your home does not have a fireplace, burn the yarrow sticks in a flat ashtray or some other fireproof container.) After the fire has died out, take your consecrated athame in your power hand and use the tip of its blade to draw in the ashes the powerful six-pointed star known as the Seal of Solomon.

Other methods of unhexing a house include the scattering of datura (poison), red pepper, hydrangea, powdered galangal, or wintergreen mixed with mint in every room and around the entire property. Be sure to start at the East side and work your way in a clockwise fashion, ending at the exact spot at which you began.

How to Make an Anti-hex Mojo Bag

In my book, *The Magick of Candleburning* (later reprinted as *Wicca Candle Magick*), I described a mojo bag as typically being "a small flannel or leather drawstring bag (usually three inches wide and four inches long) that is filled with various magickal items and carried or worn as a charm to attract or dispel certain influences." Mojo bags, which are a mainstay of Hoodoo folk magick, can either be worn on a belt or a string around the neck or carried in a purse or a pocket. Recharge a mojo bag with magickal energy once a month during the appropriate planetary hour and phase of the moon, and never allow anyone other than yourself or members of your coven to handle your mojo bag, open it, or peer inside of it, or it will lose much, if not all, of its magickal potency.

On a Saturday evening when the waning moon is visible in the sky above, light a new purple candle that has been anointed with three drops of Saturn Oil or any other occult oil designed to break and protect against hexes and curses. By the light of this candle fill a purple mojo bag with a pinch of dirt from a fresh grave; a piece of mandrake root; a bit of fur clipped from the tail of an all-black cat; a black feather from a raven, crow, or black-bird; and a Pentagram of Solomon talisman (see illustration that follows). As each of the five magickal items is added to the bag, concentrate upon the goal of your spell and repeat the following rhyming incantation of enchantment:

> *By the power of tetragrammaton,*
> *By the power of this magick verse,*
> *By the power of the pentacle,*
> *Let toucheth me no hex or curse.*
> *Harming none by spell or chant,*
> *The seeds of magick now I plant.*
> *As it is willed, so mote it be!*

Seal the mojo bag and then anoint it with three drops of Saturn Oil. For maximum effectiveness, wear the bag on a string or chain around your neck, or carry it in your pocket or purse to keep yourself protected from the hexes of enemies.

A Pentagram of Solomon talisman.

Hex-breaking by Root and Flower

To break hexes and curses many Witches burn a ginseng root, a vetivert root, or a bit of dried juniper while visualizing their intents and reciting their incantations. The ginseng has been used in all manners of Chinese spellcrafting since ancient times and is regarded as one of the most magickal of all plants in the Orient.

The ague root, which is also known as unicorn root, is used by many Witches in uncrossing rituals. Take a root that has been dried in the sun, and, using a mortar and pestle, grind it into a powder and then sprinkle it around your home. This will help to keep your family and property safeguarded against an enemy's black magick. An ague root can also be carried in a mojo bag to keep evil forces at bay.

According to *Cunningham's Encyclopedia of Magical Herbs*, "Bamboo is used to break hexes, either by carrying it in a sachet, growing a plant near the house, or crushing the wood to a powder (called bamba wood) and burning." A protective magickal symbol, such as a pentagram or a Seal of Solomon, carved on a piece of bamboo is said to serve as a potent amulet to keep a person's home safe from the workings of black magick.

To rid yourself of a curse and return it to the sender, erect an altar when the moon is waning. At each end, place a black candle, and in the center, place a vase containing some snapdragons. Arrange a mirror directly behind the flowers so that the snapdragons are reflected in the glass. Light the candles and then will the sorcery and all of its negativity back to the spellcaster who cursed you.

To bring an end to any evil spell that has been placed upon you, do any of the following: stuff a hex-breaking poppet with thistles, bite into a leek and eat it, or make an infusion from either mimosa or rue and then sponge it upon your body by the light of a purple candle when the moon is waning.

An infusion made from the bark of the wahoo plant is said to rid an individual of all curses when rubbed on his or her forehead while the word "wahoo!" is shouted seven times. Handle wahoo with care and do not ingest any part of the plant or drink any infusions made from it. It is poisonous!

In addition to the other herbs mentioned throughout this chapter, the following herbs are said to be highly effective in both breaking and repelling curses when carried in a mojo bag: lady's slipper, snakeroot, snapdragon seeds, squill (also known as a sea-onion), and toadflax. To make the power of the mojo bag even more potent, combine one, two, or more of the herbs and/or add other magickal items to the bag.

The Lime Spell

To break any curse that has been placed upon you, you will need a fresh lime and 13 pins, needles, and/or sharp nails.

When the moon is waning, light a new purple candle and then, at your altar in the center of a clockwise-cast circle, pierce the lime with the 13 pins, needles, or nails. With each piercing, repeat the following incantation:

> *To break a curse, this lime I pierce,*
> *I now reverse a spell so fierce.*
> *Magick of black, I send thee back!*
> *Evil spell, returneth to hell!*
> *By power of bewitchment spoken,*
> *By power of my will, be broken!*
> *So mote it be!*

The final step is to dig a deep hole in the earth (at least three miles away from your property), cast the pierced lime into it, and then fill it in with dirt. Take your consecrated athame in your power hand and, using the tip of its blade, trace the powerful symbol of the Banishing Pentagram in the air above the spot where the lime is buried.

The web of evil that has been spun around you will begin to unravel as the buried lime begins to decay.

Binding by Ice: A Modern Witch's Spell

To render a sorcerer or sorceress powerless to inflict evil upon you through magick of any form, fashion a clay doll to represent the evil-doer. If you are able to obtain any of his or her hair, fingernail clippings, or threads from clothing, do so at once and add them to the clay because this will make your binding spell all the more powerful. If you have a photograph of the person, cut out his or her face and attach it to the face of the clay doll. But if all you have to work with is the person's name, then take in your power hand a pin, needle, nail, or nut pick and scratch the name into the body of the clay doll. Include the person's birth date and other astrological information if you know it.

Lay the clay doll upon your altar, along with a piece of black velvet or satin and a length of black cord. Light two black altar candles and, upon a hot charcoal block in an incense burner, burn some frankincense or dried rosemary. Take the clay doll in your hands and hold it over the rising smoke as you "baptize" it by saying the following words:

> By the power of the ancient gods who ruled
>   both earth and man
> Before the Birth of Christ or the shedding of
>   His blood,
> By the power of the dark Forces of nature and
>   of all the dark Creatures of the night,
> I name thee and transform thee into [name of
>   person you wish to bind].
> Be now he (she) in all thought and feeling,
> And be now powerless to resist that which I
>   commandeth!

Wrap the clay doll in the black velvet or satin, and then take the black cord and tie it three times around the doll and knot it. As you do this, say:

I bind thee once,
I bind thee twice,
With cord of black
I bind thee thrice!

The final step is to place the clay doll in your freezer, preferably somewhere in the back where it will be out of view and remain undisturbed. Concentrate upon the goal of your spell as you recite the following, and final, incantation:

By air of 32 degrees
I paralyze thee with a freeze.
I bind all of thy evil ways
For all thy nights
And all thy days.
As it is willed, so mote it be!

Afterword

I t is my sincere hope that this book has been instrumental in guiding you through the basics of magickal theory and practice, and in preparing you for the next step as you embark upon your enchanted path to magickal mysteries and spiritual enlightenment.

If you haven't already begun writing a Book of Shadows consisting of your own personal spells and/or those written by others, I strongly suggest that you start one as soon as possible. A Book of Shadows is a blank book in which a Witch records his or her magickal workings and experiences. It is common for a Book of Shadows to include rituals and Sabbat outlines; symbols (magickal, runic, astrological, and so forth); recipes for home-made incense, oils, and potions; divination methods; and information pertaining to such things as deities, magickal correspondences, and lunar phases. Basically, a Book of Shadows is a collection of any information that a Witch may find to be interesting or useful.

A coven may share a co-written Book of Shadows, which is traditionally presided over by the High Priestess (or, in some cases, the High Priest). In some cases each coven member may keep his or her own personal, handwritten copy of the coven's master copy. In addition to magickal information, a coven's Book of Shadows often includes records of coven meetings and esbats, Sabbat rites, coven policies, Wiccan laws and ethics, a directory of members, and so forth.

According to Rosemary Ellen Guiley's *The Encyclopedia of Witches and Witchcraft,* "A Book of Shadows reflects the practices and beliefs of each individual coven and the interests or specialties of the individual Witch." Traditionally, a Witch's Book of Shadows should be written by hand. Some people even feel the need to keep their Book of Shadows hidden away under lock and key, allowing no other person to touch it or even read its contents. Others are less secretive, keeping it on their altars and sometimes even casting their spells atop it.

Burning a Book of Shadows and burying its ashes in the earth upon the death of its creator is an old Pagan custom that many Witch families and covens continue to observe. In some traditions, a deceased Witch's Book of Shadows is passed down to his or her surviving children, High Priestess, or High Priest.

Any blank book, notebook, or diary can be used for a Book of Shadows. Most occult shops and metaphysical bookstores carry a wide selection of books of shadows, ranging from the simple to the leather-bound to the ornate. Many have covers decorated with pentacles or mystical designs such as runes, Celtic knotwork, dragons, unicorns, and so forth. How simple or fancy one's Book of Shadows is depends entirely upon the individual's person taste.

It is said that over time, as a Witch adds more material to his or her Book of Shadows and its contents expand, the book becomes more magickally potent.

If you desire to invoke a Pagan deity to oversee your Book of Shadows, I recommend the ancient Egyptian god Thoth. Known as The Lord of the Divine Books and depicted in works of art as an ibis-headed (sometimes baboon-headed) man with a pen-and-ink holder, Thoth is a god who presides over magick, writing, learning, astrology, and all mystical wisdom.

After learning the basics of spellcrafting and starting a Book of Shadows, my advice to novice Witches wishing to continue their studies is to learn all that they can about Witchcraft (both of the past and the present) by reading as many books as possible. I recommend just about any book written by Sybil Leek (especially *Diary of a Witch*), Scott Cunningham, Doreen Valiente, and Raymond Buckland (especially *Buckland's Complete Book of Witchcraft*). I also recommend the following titles:

The Witch's Circle, by Maria Kay Simms (Llewellyn, 1994).

The Wiccan Mysteries, by Raven Grimassi (Llewellyn, 1997).

Mastering Witchcraft, by Paul Huson (G.P. Putnam's Sons, 1970).

The Magickal Year, by Diana Ferguson (Samuel Weiser, 1996).

The Encyclopedia of Witches and Witchcraft, by Rosemary Ellen Guiley (Facts on File, 1989).

Creed of Iron, by Ron McVan (Fourteen Word Press, 1997).

The Complete Book of Amulets and Talismans and *The Complete Book of Spells, Ceremonies and Magic,* both by Migene Gonzalez-Wippler (Llewellyn, 1997).

Cat Spells, by Claire Nahmad (Gramercy, 1998).

Way of the Witch, by Lady Brenda (cassette tapes, Brenda Matarazzo, 1997).

Refer to this book's Bibliography for further study.

Web sites, lectures, and workshops are also excellent sources of information for the student of the spellcrafting arts. Some Witches prefer to study on their own, although others find that working with a study group, a coven, or even another novice suits them better. There are also some elders in the Craft who will take students under their wings, provided that the student is sincere in his or her quest for arcane knowledge. (Finding a willing elder to be one's mentor is seldom an easy task to accomplish; however, there is an old saying, "When the student is ready, a teacher will come.")

The Internet, Pagan festivals and gatherings, occult shops, metaphysical bookstores, and open circles sponsored by Pagan organizations are excellent places to meet others of a like mind. There are also many online clubs where magickally minded individuals can interact with each other and learn about the Craft. On Yahoo alone there are literally hundreds of clubs for those interested in spells, Witchcraft, Wicca, and Paganism. Among them are two of my own clubs: Gerina Dunwich's Cauldron and The Pagan Poets Society. (See the About the Author section in the back of this book for the URLs.)

In addition, there are many Pagan newsletters and periodicals (such as *Circle Network News*) that provide networking services for the Wiccan/Pagan community. Many Witches, covens, and study groups have been brought together by a classified ad placed in such a publication.

And last, but certainly not least, there are a number of schools throughout the United States and other countries that offer courses in Witchcraft, the magickal arts, and other esoteric teachings. Many of these schools offer correspondence courses for students who wish to learn in the privacy and comfort of their own homes. Some also offer classroom instruction in addition to, or in place of, home study courses.

To find a school that offers courses in Witchcraft, I suggest connecting to a Pagan search engine on the Internet (such as *www.avatarsearch.com* or *www.witchvox.com*) and then typing in the key word "school."

Two of the oldest and most highly respected Witchcraft schools in the United States are Our Lady of Enchantment (established 1980) and Gavin and Yvonne Frost's Church and School of Wicca (established 1968). Their addresses are as follows:

Our Lady of Enchantment Seminary of Wicca
P.O. Box 1366
39 Amherst Street
Nashua, NH 03061
Phone: (603) 880-7237
www.wiccaseminary.org

Church and School of Wicca
P.O. Box 297
Hinton, WV 25951
Phone: (800) 407-6660 or (304) 466-2613
Fax: (304) 466-1353
www.wicca.org

May the Old Ones guide you well on your magickal and spiritual path, and may you find the truth that you seek. Always listen to your dreams and to the signs written in the stars, and allow your intuition to be your guiding light. Follow that which is in your heart and never consent to doing anything that you feel to be not right. Harm none, and blessed be!

Resources

AzureGreen (formerly Abyss)
P.O. Box 48
Middlefield, MA 01243
Phone: (413) 623-2155
Fax: (413) 623-2156
www.Azuregreen.com

Earth Spirit Emporium
P.O. Box 181088
Utica, MI 48318
Phone: (810) 323-8918
http://earthspirit.theshop.com

E-Witch Pagan Auction (buy/sell/barter)
www.e-witch.com
e-mail: *EclecticAuction@e-witch.com*

Gypsy Heaven
115 S. Main Street
New Hope, PA 18938

House of Avalon/Papa Jim
5630 S. Flores Street
San Antonio, TX 78214

The Magical Blend/Le Melange Magique
1928 St. Catherine Street West
Montreal, Quebec, Canada H3H-IM4
Phone: (514) 938-1458
www.themagicalblend.com

Miller's Rexall
87 Broad Street
Atlanta, GA 30303
Phone: (404) 523-8481
www.millersrexall.com

OccultBooks.com
www.occultbooks.com
e-mail: *suggest@occultbooks.com*

Occult-Shop.com
Phone: (800) 433-6459
Voice mail: (732) 295-7550
www.occult-shop.com/witchcraft.htm

Panpipes Magickal Marketplace
1641Cahuenga Boulevard
Hollywood, CA 90028
Phone: (323) 462-7078
Fax: (323) 462-6700
www.Panpipes.com

The Pyramid Collection
Altid Park, P.O. Box 3333
Chelmsford, MA 01824
Phone: (800) 333-4220
www.pyramidcollection.com

Serpents Occult Books
P.O. Box 290644
Pt. Orange, FL 32129
Phone: (904) 760-7675
www.abebooks.com/home/serpentsbooks

For a complete list of metaphysical shops and mail order companies, Witchcraft schools, Wiccan churches, covens, Pagan periodicals, and organizations, see my book, *The Wicca Source Book,* revised edition.

Bibliography

Almond, Jocelyn, and Keith Seddon. *Understanding Tarot.* London: The Aquarian Press, 1991.

Berger, Helen A. *A Community of Witches.* Columbia, S.C.: University of South Carolina Press, 1999.

Bowes, Susan. *Notions and Potions.* New York: Sterling Publishing Company, 1997.

Buckland, Raymond. *Gypsy Witchcraft and Magic.* St. Paul: Llewellyn Publications, 1998.

———. *Practical Candleburning Rituals.* St. Paul: Llewellyn Publications, 1970.

Budge, E.A. Wallis. *Amulets and Superstitions.* New York: Dover Publications, 1978.

Cunningham, Scott. *Cunningham's Encyclopedia of Magical Herbs.* St. Paul: Llewellyn Publications, 1985.

Dale-Green, Patricia. *Cult of the Cat.* Boston: Houghton Mifflin, 1963.

DeVore, Nicholas. *Encyclopedia of Astrology.* New York: Philosophical Library, 1947.

Dey, Charmaine. *The Magic Candle.* Plainview, N.Y.: Original Publications, 1982.

Farrar, Stewart. *What Witches Do.* Index, Wash.: Phoenix Publishing, 1989.

Gonzalez-Wippler, Migene. *The Complete Book of Spells, Ceremonies, and Magic.* St. Paul: Llewellyn Publications, 1988.

———. *The Complete Book of Amulets and Talismans.* St. Paul: Llewellyn Publications, 1991.

Gray, Eden. *The Complete Guide to the Tarot.* New York: Crown Publishers, 1970.

Guiley, Rosemary Ellen. *The Encyclopedia of Witches and Witchcraft.* New York: Facts on File, 1989.

Huson, Paul. *Mastering Witchcraft.* New York: G.P. Putnam's Sons, 1970.

Knight, Gareth. *The Magical World of the Tarot: Fourfold Mirror of the Universe.* York Beach, Maine: Samuel Weiser, 1996.

Leek, Sybil. *The Sybil Leek Book of Fortune Telling.* Toronto: Macmillan, 1969.

———. *Sybil Leek's Book of Curses.* Englewood Cliffs, N.J.: Prentice-Hall, 1975.

Lucas, Richard. *The Magic of Herbs in Daily Living.* West Nyack, N.Y.: Parker Publishing, 1972.

Martello; Leo L. *Understanding the Tarot.* New York: Castle Books, 1972.

————. *Black Magic, Satanism, and Voodoo.* Secaucus, N.J.: Castle Books, 1973.

Opie, Iona, and Moira Tatem, eds. *A Dictionary of Superstitions.* New York: Oxford University Press, 1989.

Pennick, Nigel. *The Pagan Book of Days.* Rochester, Vt.: Destiny Books, 1992.

Pickering, David. *Dictionary of Superstitions.* London: Cassell, 1995.

Shaw, Eva. *Divining the Future.* New York: Facts on File, 1995.

Solomon, Maria. *Helping Yourself With Magickal Oils A-Z.* Plainview, N.Y.: Original Publications, 1997.

Struthers, Jane. *Predicting Your Future: The Complete Book of Divination.* London: Collins and Brown, 1997.

Valiente, Doreen. *An ABC of Witchcraft Past and Present.* New York: St. Martin's Press, 1973.

Waite, Arthur Edward. *The Pictorial Key to the Tarot.* Secaucus, N.J.: Citadel Press, 1990.

Walker, Barbara G. *The Woman's Encyclopedia of Myths and Secrets.* Edison, N.J.: Castle Books, 1983.

Walker, Charles. *The Encyclopedia of the Occult.* New York: Crescent Books, 1995.

Wedeck, Harry E. *Treasury of Witchcraft.* New York: Philosophical Library, 1961.

Wilson, Colin. *The Occult.* New York: Random House, 1971.

Index

Abracadabra, 86
Air, 17-18
Altar bell, 15
Altar candles, 102-103
Amulet, cat's eye, 196-197
Amulets,
    gypsy, 82-83
    man-made, 79-82
    natural, 82
Anise, 154-155
Astral candles, 103-105
Astrological correspondences, 36-38
Athame, 12

Basil, 155
Bast-Wicca Tradition, 121-125
Bay, 155-156
Beltane anti-disease
    spell, 112-113
Beltane, 52
Black cat–shaped, 108-109
Black magick, 183-205
Blood-magick, 120-121

Book of Shadows, writing, 206
Bread spells, 114
Brooms, 147-149

Calendar correspondences, 34-35
Candle
    fertility spell, 131-132
    history, 92-98
    magick, 92-109
    ritual, hex-breaking, 197-198
    spell, Yule, 172
Candlemas, 50-51
    spells, 112
Candles
    and dreams, 97
    and the dead, 96
    and the Devil, 96
Candles,
    altar, 102-103
    astral, 103-105
    birthday, 97-98
    black cat-shaped, 108-109
    Devil-shaped, 108
    double-action, 105-107

dressing before a ritual, 100-102
human image, 107
Novena, 105
offertory, 105
   types of, 105-109
separation, 107
seven-knob, 105
skull-shaped, 107-108
triple-action, 107
types used in candle
   magick, 102-109
Voodoo, 98
Capers, 156-157
Caraway, 157
Cat's eye amulet, 196-197
Catnip, 157-158
Cauldron divination, 119-120
Cauldron, 14
Chalice, 14-15
Chamomile, 158
Chariot card, the, 68-69
Charms, 84-86
Cherry stone love spell, 115-116
Christians and spellcrafting, 26-27
Cinnamon, 158-159
Cloves, 159
Coffin nails, 117-118
Color correspondences, 33-34
Cord, 14
Corn doll, 113-114
Correspondences,
   astrological, 36-38
   calendar, 34-35
   color, 33-34
   lunar, 35-36
   magickal, 32-38
   talismanic, 88-91
Countermagick, 17th-century, 198
Crystal ball, spell to enchant, 54
Cumin, 159
Curses, 185-189

Dark moon, 43
Death card, 72
Deities, kitchen, 144-145
Devil, the, 9, 25-26, 93, 96
   and candles, 96
Devil-shaped candles, 108
Dill, 159-160
Divination, 61-77
Double-action candles, 105-107
Dreams, 97

Earth, 19-20
Easter fertility spell, 131
Eclipses, 44
Elemental spells, 45
Elements,
   presence of in the kitchen, 145
   working in harmony with, 17-20
Emperor card, the, 67
Empress card, the, 66-67

Fall Equinox, 53
Fertility
   deities, Pagan, 130-131
   magick, 126-132
Fetishes, 83-84
Fire, 18-19
Fool card, the, 64-65
Full moon, 41-42

Garlic, 160
Ginger, 160-161

Halloween wishbone
   divination, 114-115
Hanged man card, the, 71
Herbs, 143
   enchanting prior to spellwork, 118
   magickal properties of, 153-167
Hermit card, the, 69-70
Hex-breaking, 202-203
Hierophant card, the, 67

High magick, 28
High Priestess card, the, 66
Human image candles, 107
Hungarian healing spell, 115

Ice, binding by, 204-205
Image candle binding spell, 193-194

Jade dragon spell, 117
Judgment card, 76-77
Justice card, 70-71

Kitchen
blessing, 144
deities, 144-145
everyday items, magickal
uses for, 147-153
omens, 145-147
magick and, 143-167
presence of Elements in, 145
Knives, 149-150

Lammas, 52-53
spells, 113-114
Leek, Sybil, 177-182
Lime spell, 203
Lord's Prayer, the, 27-28
Love magick, 22
ethics of, 20-21
Love-drawing bath, 116
Lovers card, the, 68
Low magick, 29
Lunar
correspondences, 35-36
magick, 40-45

Mace, 161
Magician card, the, 65
Magick, 22
and the kitchen, 143-167
Magick,
black, 183-205

blood, 120-121
candle, 92-109
fertility, 126-132
high, 28
love, 20-21
low, 29
lunar, 40-45
Magickal
correspondences, 32-38
objects, 78-91
oils, 194-196
Major Arcana, the 22 keys of
the, 63-64
Marjoram, 161
Medical Alchemy, 55-56
Mint, 161-162
Mirror spell, 192-193
Mistletoe
love divination, 175
love spell, 174
luck spell, 171-172
Mojo bag, making an
antihex, 200-201
Money-attracting spell, 119
Moon card, the, 75-76
Moon,
dark, 43
full, 41-42
new, 40
void-of-course, 34
waning, 43
waxing, 41
Mother Goddess, ritual to honor, 111
Mustard, 162

New moon, 40
Nightmares, 187
Novena candles, 105
Nutmeg, 162-163

Offertory candles, 105
types of, 105-109

Oregano, 163

Parchments, 109
Parsley, 163
Pentacle, 13, 83
Pepper, 164
Planetary hours of the day (chart), 59
Planetary hours of the night (chart), 60
Planetary hours, 55-57
   calculating, 56-57
Poppet spell, 192
Poppy seeds, 164
Pots and pans, 152-153
Power hand, 28
Purple candle spell, 191-192

Rain spell, 139-140

Saffron, 164
Sage, 164-165
Saint Agnes' Day, 50
Saint Valentine's Day, 51
Salt, 150-152
Samhain, 53-54
Separation candles, 107
Sesame seeds, 165
Seven-knob candles, 105
Skull-shaped candles, 107-108
Spearmint, 165
Spellcasting, frequently asked questions about, 22-31
Spellcraft, tools of, 11-15
Spells for the new year, 110-111
Spells,
   crafting your own, 15-16
   Elemental, 45
Spices, magickal properties of, 153-167
Spring Equinox, 51-52
Star card, the, 74-75

Strength card, the, 69
Summer Solstice, 52
Sun card, the, 76
Sword, 13

Talismanic correspondences, 88-91
Talismans, 86-91
Tarot incantation, 63-64
Tarot, 62-77, 187
Tarragon, 166
Three Powers, the, 22
Threefold Law, the, 29-31
Thyme, 166
Timing, 39-60
Tools of spellcraft, 11-15
Tower card, the, 74
Triple-action candles, 107
Turmeric, 166-167
Void-of-course moon, 43

Wand, 12-13
Waning moon, 43
Water, 19
Waxing moon, 41
Weatherworking, 133-141
   in the name of God, 138-139
Wheel of Fortune card, the, 70
Winter Solstice, 54
Witch Bottle, 199-200
Witch's milk, 129-130
Witching hour, the, 45-49
   the, folklore surrounding, 47-49
World card, the, 77

Yule, 168-177
   cake luck spell, 173
   candle spell, 172
   pudding spell, 171
   superstitions, 169-170
Yuletide spellcraft, 171-173

About the Author

G erina Dunwich (whose first name is pronounced "Jereena") is a practicing Witch, an ordained minister (Universal Life Church), and a respected spokesperson for the Pagan community. She considers herself to be a lifelong student of the occult and is the author of more than a dozen books on the spellcasting arts and the earth-oriented religion of Wicca. Her most popular titles include *The Wicca Spellbook*, *Wicca A to Z*, *Wicca Candle Magick*, *Everyday Wicca*, *The Wicca Source Book*, and *Wicca Love Spells*. Her books have been translated into many languages in many countries.

Born under the sign of Capricorn, Gerina is also a professional astrologer and Tarot reader whose clients include many Hollywood celebrities and fellow occult authors. She is the founder of The Wheel of Wisdom School and the Pagan Poets Society, a poet, and a cat-lover. She writes and plays music and has lived in various parts of the world, including a 300-year-old

Colonial house near Salem, Massachusetts, and a haunted Victorian mansion in upstate New York. Her interests include herbal folklore, mythology, spiritualism, divination, dreamwork, hypnotism, and past-life regression. Gerina currently lives in the Los Angeles area with her Gemini soul mate and their feline familiars.

Gerina Dunwich's Web sites

The Mystical, Magickal World of Gerina Dunwich

www.wicca.drak.net/dunwich

Gerina Dunwich's Cauldron

clubs.yahoo.com/clubs/gerinadunwichscauldron

Gerina's Grimoire

iamawitch.com/freepages/grimoire

The Pagan Poets Society

clubs.yahoo.com/clubs/paganpoetssociety